DISCARD

# Garbage and Recycling

## Opposing Viewpoints®

# Other Books of Related Interest

# Garbage and Recycling

## Opposing Viewpoints®

Helen Cothran, *Book Editor*

Daniel Leone, *President*
Bonnie Szumski, *Publisher*
Scott Barbour, *Managing Editor*

OPPOSING
VIEWPOINTS®
SERIES

GREENHAVEN
PRESS®

THOMSON
———————*———————
GALE

San Diego • Detroit • New York • San Francisco • Cleveland
New Haven, Conn. • Waterville, Maine • London • Munich

*For more information, contact*
Greenhaven Press
27500 Drake Rd.
Farmington Hills, MI 48331-3535
Or you can visit our Internet site at http://www.gale.com

**LIBRARY OF CONGRESS CATALOGING-IN-PUBLICATION DATA**

Garbage and recycling : opposing viewpoints / by Helen Cothran, book editor.
   p. cm. — (Opposing viewpoints series)
Includes bibliographical references and index.
Contents: Is garbage a serious problem?—Is recycling effective?—Is toxic waste disposal a serious problem?—What innovations will help reduce waste?
ISBN 0-7377-1229-5 (pbk. : alk. paper) —
ISBN 0-7377-1230-9 (hardback : alk. paper)
   1. Refuse and refuse disposal—Juvenile literature. 2. Recycling (Waste, etc.)—Juvenile literature. 3. Hazardous wastes—Juvenile literature. [1. Refuse and refuse disposal. 2. Recycling (Waste) 3. Hazardous wastes.] I. Cothran, Helen. II. Opposing viewpoints series (Unnumbered)
TD792 .G37 2003
363.72'8—dc21
          2002000379

Printed in the United States of America

"Congress shall make
no law...abridging the
freedom of speech, or of
the press."

*First Amendment to the U.S. Constitution*

The basic foundation of our democracy is the First
Amendment guarantee of freedom of expression.
The Opposing Viewpoints Series is dedicated to the
concept of this basic freedom and the idea that it is
more important to practice it than to enshrine it.

# Contents

# Why Consider Opposing Viewpoints?

*"The only way in which a human being can make some approach to knowing the whole of a subject is by hearing what can be said about it by persons of every variety of opinion and studying all modes in which it can be looked at by every character of mind. No wise man ever acquired his wisdom in any mode but this."*

John Stuart Mill

In our media-intensive culture it is not difficult to find differing opinions. Thousands of newspapers and magazines and dozens of radio and television talk shows resound with differing points of view. The difficulty lies in deciding which opinion to agree with and which "experts" seem the most credible. The more inundated we become with differing opinions and claims, the more essential it is to hone critical reading and thinking skills to evaluate these ideas. Opposing Viewpoints books address this problem directly by presenting stimulating debates that can be used to enhance and teach these skills. The varied opinions contained in each book examine many different aspects of a single issue. While examining these conveniently edited opposing views, readers can develop critical thinking skills such as the ability to compare and contrast authors' credibility, facts, argumentation styles, use of persuasive techniques, and other stylistic tools. In short, the Opposing Viewpoints Series is an ideal way to attain the higher-level thinking and reading skills so essential in a culture of diverse and contradictory opinions.

In addition to providing a tool for critical thinking, Opposing Viewpoints books challenge readers to question their own strongly held opinions and assumptions. Most people form their opinions on the basis of upbringing, peer pressure, and personal, cultural, or professional bias. By reading carefully balanced opposing views, readers must directly confront new ideas as well as the opinions of those with whom they disagree. This is not to simplistically argue that everyone who reads opposing views will—or should—change his or her opinion. Instead, the series enhances readers' understanding of their own views by encouraging confrontation with opposing ideas. Careful examination of others' views can lead to the readers' understanding of the logical inconsistencies in their own opinions, perspective on why they hold an opinion, and the consideration of the possibility that their opinion requires further evaluation.

## Evaluating Other Opinions

To ensure that this type of examination occurs, Opposing Viewpoints books present all types of opinions. Prominent spokespeople on different sides of each issue as well as well-known professionals from many disciplines challenge the reader. An additional goal of the series is to provide a forum for other, less known, or even unpopular viewpoints. The opinion of an ordinary person who has had to make the decision to cut off life support from a terminally ill relative, for example, may be just as valuable and provide just as much insight as a medical ethicist's professional opinion. The editors have two additional purposes in including these less known views. One, the editors encourage readers to respect others' opinions—even when not enhanced by professional credibility. It is only by reading or listening to and objectively evaluating others' ideas that one can determine whether they are worthy of consideration. Two, the inclusion of such viewpoints encourages the important critical thinking skill of objectively evaluating an author's credentials and bias. This evaluation will illuminate an author's reasons for taking a particular stance on an issue and will aid in readers' evaluation of the author's ideas.

It is our hope that these books will give readers a deeper understanding of the issues debated and an appreciation of the complexity of even seemingly simple issues when good and honest people disagree. This awareness is particularly important in a democratic society such as ours in which people enter into public debate to determine the common good. Those with whom one disagrees should not be regarded as enemies but rather as people whose views deserve careful examination and may shed light on one's own.

Thomas Jefferson once said that "difference of opinion leads to inquiry, and inquiry to truth." Jefferson, a broadly educated man, argued that "if a nation expects to be ignorant and free . . . it expects what never was and never will be." As individuals and as a nation, it is imperative that we consider the opinions of others and examine them with skill and discernment. The Opposing Viewpoints Series is intended to help readers achieve this goal.

David L. Bender and Bruno Leone,
Founders

---

Greenhaven Press anthologies primarily consist of previously published material taken from a variety of sources, including periodicals, books, scholarly journals, newspapers, government documents, and position papers from private and public organizations. These original sources are often edited for length and to ensure their accessibility for a young adult audience. The anthology editors also change the original titles of these works in order to clearly present the main thesis of each viewpoint and to explicitly indicate the opinion presented in the viewpoint. These alterations are made in consideration of both the reading and comprehension levels of a young adult audience. Every effort is made to ensure that Greenhaven Press accurately reflects the original intent of the authors included in this anthology.

---

# Introduction

*"They live in the closet like ghosts of simpler times. Dead monitors. Obsolete PCs. Fried printers. A lot of junk has collected after 20 years of the PC."*

—*P.J. Huffstutter, technology writer for the* Los Angeles Times

Computers have revolutionized the way that work gets done. Assembly lines have become automated, banks have installed ATMs, and libraries now provide online card catalogs. Although most people living in developed countries take computers for granted and believe that they are beneficial, many analysts point out that there is a downside to computers: They generate waste and pollution.

As most computer owners know, computers become obsolete quickly. Because ever-improving software programs require faster and more powerful hardware to run them, consumers who wish to use the latest applications must purchase new machines. As John Yaukey of the Gannett News Service quips, "Computers . . . are obsolete 18 months after they're out of the bubble wrap." P.J. Huffstutter, reporting for the *Los Angeles Times*, explains that "in 1998 alone, about 21 million personal computers became obsolete in the United States." By 2005, 350 million machines will have reached obsolescence, according to the National Safety Council. At least 55 million of those computers are expected to end up in landfills, which some analysts say will be inadequate for storing the increasing amounts of waste created during the computer age.

Finding space to dispose of obsolete machines is not the only environmental problem computers pose. Many analysts contend that the toxic components inside computers and the hazardous waste generated by the manufacturing of the machines are threatening human health. According to Molly O'Meara, writing for *USA Today* magazine, "the lead in monitors, the mercury and chromium in central processing units, and the arsenic and halogenated organic substances inside the devices all become health hazards." Such toxics, when disposed of improperly, can leach into groundwater, contaminating municipal water supplies. The Silicon Valley Toxics Coalition, a grassroots organization that monitors the pollution generated by computer production, has created maps showing increasing pollution from semi-conductor manufacturing in Northern California. The maps indicate sources of toxic chemical releases and hazardous waste sites surrounding the San Francisco Bay area. As of 2000, the U.S. Environmental Protection Agency was monitoring twenty-nine such sites in Silicon Valley alone. According to the Clean Computer Campaign, workers in chip manufacturing in Silicon Valley have reported cancer clusters and birth defects.

Many environmentalists point out that computer use also results in increased industrial pollution. For example, computers use electricity, which is generated by burning fossil fuels, a process that creates greenhouse gases that many think contribute to global warming. Computer users also discard large quantities of paper. Making virgin paper requires cutting down trees and processing the pulp at paper mills, which generate pollution. Many experts predict that the paper disposal problem is getting worse. According to O'Meara, between 1988 and 1998, average consumption of printing and writing paper increased by 24 percent.

Not everyone takes such a dim view of computers, however. In fact, optimists predict that future improvements in computer technology will result in less overall energy consumption, waste, and pollution. Proponents predict that computers will enable people to work from home, thereby reducing the use of energy for transportation. They also claim that more energy will be saved as consumers shop more often via the Internet, which will reduce the number of trips made to stores. Fewer car trips overall will result in a reduction of dangerous auto emissions.

Computer defenders maintain that advances in computer technology will result in less waste, as well. They believe that improvements in monitor designs will make screens easier to read and reduce the use of paper for printing hard copies. Since less paper will be used, fewer trees will need to be cut down and fewer pollutants will be generated by paper mills. Other important developments will be improvements in computer recycling processes that will reduce the amount of toxic components that must be disposed of. Many commentators point out that computers can also make it easier for environmentalists around the world to exchange information and help activists work together to solve environmental problems.

In many ways, computers highlight America's garbage problems in general. After all, computers are not the only consumer products that become outdated quickly: consumers are constantly upgrading to bigger televisions, buying late-model automobiles, and replacing old appliances with new ones. Indeed, many analysts contend that Americans live a "throwaway lifestyle." They point out that the U.S. economy is based on consumption, but consumption—by its nature—produces waste. As consumption increases, so does the amount of garbage that needs to be disposed of. To be sure, as producers continue to produce and consumers continue to consume, more strategies will be needed to deal with an increasing amount of waste.

While most people give little thought to where their discarded computers and other consumer products wind up, scientists, policy makers, activists, and industry leaders work behind the scenes to make garbage disposal as safe and inexpensive as possible. Of course, how best to accomplish that goal continues to be a source of contention. The authors in *Garbage and Recycling: Opposing Viewpoints* discuss various garbage problems and debate waste disposal options in the following chapters: Is Garbage a Serious Problem? Is Recycling Effective? Is Toxic Waste Disposal a Serious Problem? What Innovations Will Help Reduce Waste? Disposing of obsolete computers safely will surely be among the topics discussed by waste management experts for years to come.

# CHAPTER 1

# Is Garbage a Serious Problem?

# Chapter Preface

At dusk on the balcony of a Princess Cruise ship, a vacation-ing couple watched as crew members tossed some twenty trash bags filled with garbage into the sea. Shocked, the couple videotaped the incident and later turned the tape over to the U.S. Department of Justice and the FBI. As a re-sult of the couple's action, the cruise line was fined $500,000 in 1993.

In some ways, cruise ships mirror American society. Pas-sengers aboard luxury liners consume large quantities of food and beverages and produce immense amounts of waste. For example, on a typical seven-day Princess Cruise, passengers consume a ton and a half of cheese, five-and-a-half tons of meat, and five hundred bottles of champagne. Any leftover food, all of the packaging, and any used plastic utensils must be discarded. Dumping refuse into the ocean is a convenient way to dispose of garbage, of course, but new international laws have made the majority of ocean dumping illegal. In-stead, cruise ships must pay to have garbage offloaded at ports-of-call or processed on the vessels themselves. These waste management activities are for the most part conducted out of sight of passengers.

Like vacationers on cruise ships, most Americans con-sume enormous amounts of resources and generate huge quantities of garbage. Like cruise ship passengers, most Americans give little thought to the trash that they generate. In most cities, homeowners simply place residential trash curbside once a week where it is picked up by garbage trucks and hauled to landfills outside city limits. Just as cruise lin-ers are transitioning to more environmentally benign ways of disposing of garbage, so too have municipalities adopted waste disposal methods such as sanitary landfills that are su-perior to methods used in the past.

Because municipal trash collection is so efficient, few people are likely to give much thought to garbage issues. Those who do often hold widely different opinions. Some people believe that garbage is not a serious problem and claim that there is plenty of landfill space left to dispose of what waste will be produced well into the future. Many residents do not participate in municipal recycling programs, arguing that they are unnecessary and inconvenient. Of course, many cruise ship passengers bring these ideas on board with them. Carnival Cruises spokesperson Jennifer de la Cruz contends that as the company began making efforts to reduce waste, passengers complained. She reports, "We get accused of being cheap because we don't provide amenities in the cabins like shampoo and conditioner. But it cuts down on those little plastic bottles."

Many individuals are concerned about garbage, however, and take steps to address what they see as a serious problem. For instance, the couple who videotaped the illegal dumping by the Princess Cruise ship helped initiate efforts to curtail garbage dumping at sea. Many homeowners recycle, buy fewer goods, and compost their household and garden waste. Others pressure government officials to clean up toxic waste sites.

Even though garbage problems remain out of sight of most individuals, politicians, environmentalists, and policy analysts argue vociferously about waste issues. Authors in the following chapter join the debate about whether garbage is a serious problem.

> *"Concerted efforts will be necessary if we are to avoid a collision course with twenty-first-century wastebergs."*

# Better Waste Management Strategies Are Needed to Avert a Garbage Crisis

Arthur H. Purcell

Arthur H. Purcell is a Los Angeles–based environmental management analyst and educator. In the following viewpoint, Purcell contends that America's consumer lifestyle wastes resources and generates an increasing amount of garbage that pollutes the environment. He claims that while waste disposal methods have improved, these advances will not be sufficient to head off a garbage crisis. Instead, new strategies to reduce the amount of waste generated will be necessary. Purcell identifies several developments—such as the emergence of environmentally friendly businesses—that promise to help the nation avoid such a crisis.

As you read, consider the following questions:
1. According to Purcell, what problems are associated with siting landfills?
2. In the author's opinion, what factors have increased efforts to separate wastes at or near their source?
3. Why are companies reluctant to reduce product packaging, as stated by the author?

Excerpted from "Trash Troubles," by Arthur H. Purcell, *World and I*, November 1998. Copyright © 1998 by News World Communications, Inc. Reprinted with permission.

Our accumulating piles of solid waste threaten to ruin our environment, pointing to the urgent need for not only better disposal methods but also strategies to lower the rate of waste generation.

## A Titanic Garbage Problem

As our ship surges forward, we notice a mound jutting up ahead, directly in our path. Like an iceberg, a much larger mass is hidden beneath the surface. If we keep running the vessel at current speed, we may have a major problem on our hands.

No, this is not the *Titanic*. The ship we're on is our consumer-goods-dependent lifestyle that creates as much as a ton of solid waste per person each year. And the peak ahead is but the tip of a massive "wasteberg" that is 95 percent hidden from view: For every ton of trash we generate, there is an underlying loss of another 19 tons of industrial, agricultural, mining, and transportation wastes, building up into a mound that threatens to shatter our future.

The wasteberg entails a formidable economic and environmental challenge. For most local governments, solid waste management ranks behind only schools and highways as the major budget item. Improperly managed solid waste eats up dollars while polluting water supplies, threatening neighborhoods, and squandering natural resources.

So how is this odyssey progressing? Are we about to capsize on the wasteberg and drown, or can we successfully circumnavigate the threat? Better yet, can we shrink the wasteberg?

## Circumnavigating the Wasteberg

The simplest way to steer around the wasteberg is to try to isolate wastes from their surrounding environment. This has been the major approach worldwide—solid waste management has usually meant solid waste disposal.

In the United States, most solid waste is placed in sanitary landfills, which are specially designed garbage burial grounds. Mixed organic and inorganic wastes are methodically placed in sections called cells, which are then covered with dirt. Drainage systems are installed to collect rainwater that has percolated through the cells and become contaminated. And wells are installed to monitor how much methane gas is produced as the wastes decompose.

At one time, landfills were little more than covered dumps, waiting to contaminate the air, land, and water around them. But through trial and error, landfill technologies have become relatively sophisticated, and landfills that promise low long-term environmental impacts are now feasible.

The siting of landfills, however, is becoming almost exponentially more difficult over time, particularly in populated areas. The reduced availability of open land, the inevitable environmental impacts of transporting waste, and the pervasive "not in my backyard" opposition to landfills have diminished the prospects for future landfills while dramatically increasing their projected costs. Most major landfill projects now on the drawing board are in remote rural locations, where the short-term economic benefits offered by landfills are valued. To use these sites, wastes have to be shipped over long distances by rail.

Around the world, many nations have chosen incineration as the preferred way to dispose of solid waste. This is particularly the case where landfill sites are scarce. Japan, for example, has around 2,800 municipal incinerators that reduce solid wastes to ashes. In the United States, though, incineration has fallen strongly out of favor. Despite significant improvements in the technology, concerns that the incineration process may release toxic pollutants such as dioxins have brought this once-popular technology to near-obsolescence.

## Shrinking the Wasteberg

For every pound of trash that goes into the waste basket, another 19 are released elsewhere in the environment—in forms ranging from industrial byproducts to fertilizer runoff to wasted energy. Thus if we reduce our generation of solid waste, the "leverage effect" is enormous: Each ton of trash kept out of the dump means that 19 tons of waste, along with related environmental impacts and the dollar cost of producing it, are avoided.

There are three major approaches to narrowing the waste stream: reducing, redesigning, and recycling. All require vigorous participation by both producers and consumers.

*Reducing.* Producers reduce waste through offering products that are less wasteful. Consumers reduce waste by using less of the product and using materials longer.

*Redesigning.* Producers offer alternative products that have a lower environmental impact than traditional ones, while continuing to meet given needs.

*Recycling.* Producers make reusable products, utilizing waste materials in manufacturing these goods. Consumers reuse the products and collect the materials to recycle out of the waste stream and back to the producers.

Until rather recently, the emphasis on reducing this country's waste focused almost solely on recycling. The consensus was that reducing or redesigning products interfered with market-based decision making. Product design and function should be left alone, it was reasoned, and waste reduction would come through recycling the leftovers.

Initial efforts in large-scale recycling led to many expensive failures. Most surveys showed that consumers did not want to presort their trash. And because recycling requires separating materials, the approach was to develop sophisticated technologies to separate mixed wastes at large central facilities.

Ultimately, however, thermodynamics and economics caused a rethinking of recycling strategies, as centralized recycling systems proved both costly and impractical. From Monsanto's Landgard system in Baltimore to American Can's Milwaukee Americology plant to the big National Center for Resource Recovery's New Orleans facility, the large-scale "high-tech" plants (as they were then called) have disappeared.

## Recycling Woes

A combination of factors has, on the other hand, led to increased efforts to separate wastes at or near their sources. These factors include increased public willingness to participate in environmentally oriented community programs, improved collection technologies (such as specially designed trucks), effectively targeted recycling campaigns, and local and state laws requiring separation. Most cities and towns across the United States now have source separation programs of some type. California's ambitious mandatory separation program is targeted to divert 50 percent of the waste stream by the early part of the next decade.

While these projects are usually labeled as recycling programs, it is important to differentiate between programs that involve separation and those that perform actual recycling. A material is not truly recycled until it is remanufactured into a new product. The perennial fluctuation of recyclable ("secondary") materials prices, combined with generally depressed virgin materials markets, means that recyclable products are sometimes virtually worthless.

Luckovich. © 1990 by Creators Syndicate. Reprinted with permission.

Paper—the major component of most solid waste—is a telling example of the limits of separation programs aimed at getting used materials back into the manufacturing stream. According to one recycling industry official, secondary paper prices have been "in solid recession for the past three years." Supply has outstripped demand. "The U.S. is collecting higher volumes of some specific grades of recovered paper than mills here can consume at current operating rates," he notes.

The "relief valve" for paper recycling, this official points out, is Asia. China, in particular, is importing massive amounts of paper. Imports of secondary newsprint, for instance, were up 23 percent for the first quarter of 1998, compared with the same period in 1997. Other recyclables have also been faring well in the Asian market. While that continent's economic turbulence in 1998 could slow down such imports, the depressed prices of most secondary materials may, conversely, make them more attractive than their virgin alternatives. The organized theft of separated curbside materials, occurring in many urban areas, can be directly attributed to the export value of recyclables.

Of the major solid wastes, glass has the least demand in recycling markets, while aluminum stands at the other end of the spectrum. Because of the unique metallurgical nature of aluminum and the high energy costs of producing it, the aluminum industry can cost-effectively recycle virtually all secondary aluminum (usually obtained in the form of discarded beverage containers).

Private-public sector partnerships have added to aluminum's recyclability. In many parts of this country, state and local governments have established mandatory beverage deposit laws, which provide a fund to compensate recyclers. At the same time, the aluminum industry has long had an aggressive buy-back program for aluminum recyclables. Motivating this program is the fact that 95 percent of the huge energy costs of smelting aluminum can be avoided through recycling. Thus aluminum recycling has long-term economic appeal.

## Landfills and Incinerators as Recycling Centers

Landfills can potentially become energy recycling facilities. Decaying organic wastes produce methane—the same gas we burn in stoves and furnaces. In principle, therefore, concentrated organic solid wastes could become sources of usable methane. A number of groups have experimented with recovering methane from landfills and selling it to utilities. But the economics of methane recovery have varied widely, depending on the quality and quantity of gas produced.

Landfills themselves are recyclable. A number of parks and recreation areas across the country—including a golf course on the upscale Palos Verdes peninsula in Southern California and the Mount Trashmore sled run in Evanston, Illinois—sit on former landfills. While "hot spots" from methane gas sometimes pose problems on this reclaimed land, they are usually controllable.

Some people envision landfills of the future as full-fledged recycling centers. Separated materials could be buried there temporarily until reclaimed as secondary resources.

Incineration, too, has a recycling dimension. While incineration destroys materials, it recovers energy. The energy obtained from a ton of trash is equivalent to that from about two barrels of fuel oil. Several experiments have demonstrated that energy can be recovered cleanly and cost-effectively through waste incineration. Union Electric Company's pilot project in St. Louis two decades ago was one such example. Outside the United States, energy recovery is a routine feature of waste incineration.

## Reduce and Redesign

The "green consumer" movement, along with increasing corporate interest in product stewardship, may hold significant implications for shrinking the size of future wastebergs. Market research consistently shows that an impressive core of about 20–30 percent of all consumers prefer lower-waste alternatives and are often willing to pay more for such products.

Many businesses have sought to take advantage of this trend, attracting customers through offering lower-waste alternatives to traditional products and services. From supermarkets that sell in bulk and encourage consumers to bring their own shopping bags to outdoor-wear makers (such as Patagonia) that incorporate the material from used plastic bottles into vests, a viable green market has developed.

Packaging is the part of the waste stream that could be most significantly reduced through redesign. It is also the most controversial. Many producers rely on packaging design as a major part of their marketing strategy. While most consumers would agree that products are overpackaged—who needs, for instance, potato chips wrapped in both a plastic bag and an aluminum-foil container—few product makers would concur. Most attempts to regulate packaging have been unsuccessful here, but some packaging standardization has been adopted in other nations.

Major changes in product form may significantly affect the size of twenty-first-century wastebergs. One intriguing example is the electronic book (or e-book)—an electronically activated, recyclable hardcover book whose text and graphics can be changed through simple downloading and uploading. Included in the purchase price of e-books (projected at $300–$2,000) will be access to hundreds of manuscripts. Hence, instead of keeping a shelf full of textbooks—which, when outdated, become throwaways—an e-book owner would have just one recyclable book.

As we approach a new millennium, we will have in place many tools for the efficient, cost-effective, and environmentally responsive management of waste. But as the "away" in "throwing away" becomes more elusive, the challenge lies in shrinking the size of the wasteberg as well as in navigating around it.

One encouraging development is that more and more corporations are minimizing waste as part of their business plans. Moreover, surveys indicate continuing strong consumer interest in low-waste products. Similarly, innovative approaches and greater flexibility on the part of environmental regulatory agencies will improve cooperation between consumers, producers, and government in shrinking waste streams. These concerted efforts will be necessary if we are to avoid a collision course with twenty-first-century wastebergs.

"Not only did we avoid a 'garbage crisis' in the 1980s, but also . . . there are significant reasons to believe that ever-increasing waste is not inevitable."

# The Garbage Crisis Has Been Averted

Marian R. Chertow

Marian R. Chertow contends in the following viewpoint that because of fears raised in the 1980s about an increasing amount of trash, measures were taken to avert a garbage crisis. According to Chertow, the solid waste industry began to develop more efficient and environmentally benign methods of disposing of waste. Marian R. Chertow is director of the Industrial Environmental Management Program at the Yale School of Forestry and Environmental Studies. In 2000 the EPA updated its analysis of municipal solid waste generation, recycling, and disposal. The EPA found that waste generation was increasing once again. For more information on this change and related trends, see Marian R. Chertow, "Pursuing Sustainable Solid Waste Management," Rio Plus Ten Assessment: United States, John Dernbach, ed., Washington, DC: Environmental Law Institute, 2002.

As you read, consider the following questions:

1. As stated by Chertow, how has the United States been addressing the sources of radioactive waste production?
2. In Chertow's opinion, what two forces influenced the expected need for more disposal capacity in the 1980s?

Excerpted from "Waste, Industrial Ecology, and Sustainability," by Marian R. Chertow, *Social Research*, Spring 1998. Copyright © 1998 by New School for Social Research. Reprinted with permission.

U.S. castoffs are trending downward. Even in categories where more waste is actually generated, less is simply discarded in favor of some type of reclamation. Not only did we avoid a "garbage crisis" in the 1980s, but also, in the late 1990s, there are significant reasons to believe that ever-increasing waste is not inevitable. For the forces of the 1980s have led to a contextual shift in how we view waste today. Seen from the new perspective offered by industrial ecology in the broader framework of sustainable development, far fewer materials need be considered waste. . . .

## A Different Picture

Over a ten-year period, we went from landfilling 83 percent of 158 million tons of municipal solid waste (131 million tons) to landfilling only 57 percent of 208 million tons (119 million tons). Nonhazardous industrial waste disposal is thought to have fallen, perhaps significantly, largely through increased reclamation rather than decreasing generation. The levels of hazardous waste projected in the 1980s never materialized and led to severe losses by companies, such as Chemical Waste Management, investing in that business. Radioactive waste production is dominated by two sources: nuclear plants and nuclear warheads. The United States has not ordered a new nuclear plant since 1979, following the Three Mile Island nuclear accident, and has actually been destroying nuclear warheads. In this case, production is down, generation is down, and disposal is down as well, although the waste management challenges of decommissioning nuclear plants should not be underestimated.

This picture is very different than the one we feared a decade ago and is typified by the saga of municipal solid waste management. Images from the nightly news of more and more garbage with no place to go struck fear in the hearts of mayors and public works directors everywhere. Children were taught that the best way to stave off the invasion of sea gulls hovering at landfills was by washing out bottles and stacking old newspapers. But the anticipated crisis did not occur. If the culminating symbol of the predicament of the 1980s was the hapless garbage barge of 1987 wandering from port to port in search of a final resting place, then the symbol of the 1990s is anti-recycling backlash as captured by the iconoclastic June 1996 cover story of the *New York Times Magazine*, "Recycling Is Garbage," by John Tierney in which recycling is attacked at its core as a waste of time.

## Analyzing the Garbage Crisis

A postmortem of the much anticipated garbage crisis and why it never overcame the nation will help explain the current state of waste affairs. First, we can examine the notion of what constitutes a crisis, drawing on a prescient essay written by political scientist Anthony Downs in 1972 called "Up and Down with Ecology: The Issue-Attention Cycle." Downs evaluates whether environmental problems fall into the same pattern he observes concerning the public's interest in other domestic issues: typically, the problem leaps into public view, captures center stage for a while, begins to fade in part because of the recognition by the public that the problem is more complex than first thought and change has significant social costs and, most often, is replaced by some other issue moving into its "crisis" phase.

Downs identifies two types of crisis: "One kind of crisis consists of a rapidly deteriorating situation moving towards a single disastrous event at some future moment. The second consists of a more gradually deteriorating situation that will eventually pass some subtle 'point of no return.'" The second definition captures an important aspect of many global environmental problems typified by global climate change. If, indeed, there are threshold meteorological events, and we somehow cross them, then we may eventually pass a "point of no return" with severe impacts on a large part of the planet. Stratospheric ozone depletion and loss of biodiversity are other environmental problems that share the potential to unalterably affect the planet as in the second meaning of crisis. Waste—or at least nonhazardous waste—is of a different character. It does not portend a point of no return and, in fact, some consider it much more a political rather than an environmental problem because many air, water, and land concerns have been effectively addressed through regulation and improved practices.

Still, the condition Downs describes as "a rapidly deteriorating situation" moving headlong toward "a single disastrous event" describes exactly what it was like to be on the front lines of the garbage wars in the mid 1980s, when I was running a state agency charged with developing waste disposal options. Many of us were driven by the sense that if the agenda we were pursuing right that minute was not successful, the day would come (in our term of office, no less) when there would simply be no place left for the next bottle cap or banana peel. Elections were won and lost over waste disputes and in many towns waste disposal constituted the single largest expenditure of the municipal budget after education.

## A Four-Stage Process

In order to evaluate this situation and to determine whether we staved it off for the short term or whether there is still a crisis looming, we can imagine a simple model of the flow of garbage as a four-stage process, as follows:

In Stage 1, the item is discarded at the site of the waste generator, and in Stage 2, it is picked up, typically, by a big truck. It may be recycled, composted, or incinerated during Stage 3, and finally the process residues from Stage 3 and nonprocessed raw waste are delivered to landfills in Stage 4.

### A Preposterous "Crisis"

The very idea that a country as vast as the United States has nowhere left to put its refuse is preposterous on its face. . . . Nor is the trash "crisis," such as it is, getting worse, notwithstanding popular perceptions fed by front-page "news analyses" (editorials). If anything, the long-term trend is toward improvement, since the market has powerful incentives to reduce the amount and volume—that is, the cost—of packaging and other general contributors to the total volume and weight of trash. And the historical experience is consistent with this; per capita, there is little evidence that the United States is producing more solid waste than was the case decades ago.

Benjamin Zycher, *Regulation*, January 9, 2001.

Pressure on disposal, the end of this four-stage process, triggered the expectation of the solid waste crisis of the 1980s. Increasing population overall and increasing waste generation per individual were two forces greatly affecting the need for more disposal capacity. At the same time, many old landfills were reaching capacity and federal and state regulators were closing down thousands more substandard landfills. This led to increasing prices and a search for disposal alternatives, which, in turn, affected each of the other stages of the process flow. Waste managers brought attention to other approaches: reducing the quantity of waste at the source, collecting waste so that it could more easily be recycled or composted, processing waste more cost effectively, and, at each stage, addressing environmental concerns.

A grassroots organizer might claim the crisis was averted by the nationwide acceptance of recycling programs. In contrast, a waste company executive might suggest that the looming crisis was forestalled by market forces: increasing demand for disposal capacity and decreasing supply of landfills created the price incentives needed by the private sector to overcome siting opposition and create new disposal capacity. Middlepeople all along the way might take credit for 1) new innovations in truck design to facilitate recycling collection; 2) the rise of material recovery facilities (MREFs)—recycling factories that provide a missing link for processing recyclables collected at curbside; or 3) brokering deals that allowed the siting of new landfills and waste-to-energy plants. All, of course, would rightfully proclaim their role in relieving the disposal crisis.

## A Neutral Assessment

A more disinterested assessment (by a neutral social scientist) would look beyond the headlines to the information available at the time. The Environmental Protection Agency (EPA) provided extensive data on the rapidly growing amount of waste being generated and also the number of landfills that were closing. States, too, counted the number of landfill sites that were closing but did not always adequately consider either the size of the sites (they were generally quite small), or the scale of new capacity in the pipeline, whether from the expansion of existing sites or the permitting of new sites. A typical statement of the period comes from the EPA's 1988 report to Congress:

Extensive reliance on land disposal for municipal solid waste has resulted in capacity shortages in some areas of the nation. Nearly three-fourths of all municipal solid waste landfills are expected to close within 15 years, with 45 percent expected to close in five years. These shortages are becoming critical in densely populated areas of the country, particularly in the Northeast. In addition to limited source reduction and recycling, other factors that appear to be contributing to the capacity problem include difficulty in siting new disposal or treatment facilities due to public concern and limited long-term planning by some State and local governments.

The dispassionate long view from Washington was readily translated into considerable alarm among political leaders at the local level, especially those engaged in trying to site new facilities over the heated objection of nearby residents. Some analysts believed that the not-in-my-backyard (NIMBY) syndrome would be the decisive factor—that the veto-power of siting opponents would not be overcome even with sufficient market incentives. While many proposed landfills and waste-to-energy plants were never built because of opposition, figures from the National Solid Waste Management Association show that some 364 new landfills were sited between 1985 and 1991. In general, the new landfills were so much larger than the old ones that fewer successful sitings were needed. Texas, for example, went from 934 active landfills in 1988 to 192 in 1995 to bury roughly the same quantity of waste.

Analytically, as we have seen, the anticipated "garbage crisis" was a disposal problem brought on in large part due to landfill closures required under the Resource Conservation and Recovery Act (RCRA). This government intervention was then followed by reasonably appropriate market responses to create new capacity. In the end, according to policy analyst Reid Lifset, "the capacity crisis was in fact a regional and local phenomenon with considerable geographic variation. The most severe problems were in the Northeast and Midwest and Florida." According to analysts of the waste industry's trade association, the current status is that "municipal solid waste disposal capacity in the US is greater than it has been for a decade, even as the total number of municipal solid waste landfills has declined."

## Many Actors Solve the Problem

Perhaps too little consideration was given to the invisible hand of the market. But, because there is a well-organized private waste industry, there was a group ready to capitalize on projected capacity shortfalls to find new business opportunities whether in collection, disposal or processing. Interestingly, the federal landfill regulations of 1991 require compliance with environmental standards that are so costly to meet that only larger landfills can achieve the economies of scale necessary to remain cost-effective. Private sector participants have been the most prepared (with the deepest pockets) to meet these standards. One of the measures currently used to determine the profitability of a waste company today is called internalization, which refers to the ability of the company to bring a high percentage of the waste it collects to its own landfills rather than face the risk or high price of using someone else's disposal facility.

There is a curious mix of public and private actors in the world of waste, with many entangled institutional relationships. First, there is the private waste industry that contracts with commercial and industrial establishments as well as with many communities to manage waste. Since it is usually municipal governments that are formally charged with responsibility to see that waste is removed, as a matter of public welfare, there is also a long tradition of public employees providing waste management services. Also, there is the role of the public. In some sense, waste is the great equalizer—all members of the public make trash and are often quick to let their elected representatives know when there are collection problems. It is reasonable to conclude that, during the capacity crisis, the mayors, city councilors, and the public at large, hurtling toward the portended single disastrous event, were unaccustomed to relying on the role private interests would play in restoring the market to some sort of equilibrium.

Finally, our neutral social scientist would comment on the value, in terms of mobilizing political activity, of the threat of a crisis. Surely, the attention brought to the garbage problem by all involved created much of the energy that led to the forces able to relieve the problem of disposal capacity. . . .

As with all environmental issues, there are still a lot of

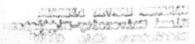

questions. Chicken and hog wastes, old problems, are threatening drinking water sources from North Carolina to Arkansas as world markets encourage production but rural and suburban land uses clash. Disposal of bioengineered wastes or wastes with millennia-long half-lives raises new issues whose possible outcomes stretch the brain. Yet, we have seen encouraging signs from consumers and producers. As recycling journalist Jerry Powell reminds us, more people recycle than vote. On the producer side, we have begun to see corporate managers move from narrow, regulatory-driven behavior to a broader emphasis on efficiency. By following the lessons of industrial ecology we need not return to the crisis days but can choose to continue to make improvements both in reclamation and process efficiency that will lead to less waste overall and more useful waste that need not be disposed.

| "*Living near a landfill is hazardous to your health.*"

# Landfills Are Dangerous

Peter Montague

Peter Montague argues in the following viewpoint that escaping landfill gases and liquids contaminate areas around most landfill sites. According to Montague, this contamination causes abnormally high incidences of cancer in people living near landfills. Other health risks associated with landfills affect children, Montague contends, including high rates of birth defects, low birth weights, and small size. Peter Montague is editor of *Rachel's Environment and Health News*, a publication of the Environmental Research Foundation.

As you read, consider the following questions:

1. According to the 1990 study cited by Montague, what percentage of California's landfills emitted one or more toxic solvents?
2. What cancers are the most commonly reported among populations living near landfills, according to the author?
3. In the author's opinion, why are solid waste landfills just as dangerous to human health as hazardous waste landfills?

A 1998 study by the New York State Department of Health reports that women living near solid waste landfills where gas is escaping have a four-fold increased chance of bladder cancer or leukemia (cancer of the blood-forming cells).

## Landfills and Cancer

The new study examined the occurrence of seven kinds of cancer among men and women living near 38 landfills where naturally occurring landfill gas is thought to be escaping into the surrounding air. Of the 14 kinds of cancer studied (7 each in men and women), 10 (or 71%) were found to be elevated but only two (bladder and leukemia in women) achieved statistical significance at the 5% level. The seven cancers studied were leukemia, non-Hodgkin's lymphoma, liver, lung, kidney, bladder, and brain cancer. In women living near landfills, the incidence of all seven kinds of cancer was elevated. In men, the study found elevated (though not statistically significant) incidence of lung cancer, bladder cancer, and leukemia.

What is most surprising about the New York study is that it only examined 38 landfills. The state Department of Health began looking at 131 landfills, but eventually studied only 38 of them (29%) on the grounds that only those 38 were likely to be releasing gases. In contrast, a 1990 study of 356 California landfills found 240 of them (or 67%) emitting one or more toxic solvents. It is not clear why New York authorities assumed that gases are escaping from only 29% of New York landfills when toxic gases have been measured escaping from 67% of the landfills tested in California.

## Toxic Landfill Gas

Landfill gas consists of naturally-occurring methane and carbon dioxide, which form inside the landfill as the waste decomposes. As the gases form, pressure builds up inside a landfill, forcing the gases to move. Some of the gases escape through the surrounding soil or simply move upward into the atmosphere, where they drift away.

Typically, landfill gases that escape from a landfill will carry along toxic chemicals such as paint thinner, solvents, pesticides, and other hazardous volatile organic compounds (VOCs), many of them chlorinated.

The New York state health department tested for VOCs escaping from 25 landfills and reported finding dry cleaning fluid (tetrachloroethylene, or PERC), trichloroethylene (TCE), toluene, 1,1,1-trichloroethane, benzene, vinyl chloride, xylene, ethylbenzene, methylene chloride, 1,2-dichloroethene, and chloroform in the escaping gases.

## Leukemia and Bladder Cancer

This is not the first study to show that people living near landfills have an increased incidence of cancer. A 1995 study of families living near a large municipal solid waste landfill (the Miron Quarry) in Montreal, Quebec, reported an elevated incidence of cancers of the stomach, liver, prostate, and lung among men, and stomach and cervix/uterus among women.

A 1984 study reported that men (but not women) living near the Drake Superfund site in Pennsylvania [where contaminated land was being remediated] had an excessive incidence of bladder cancers, though occupational exposures could not be ruled out as the source of those cancers.

A 1990 study found an increased incidence of bladder cancers in northwestern Illinois where a landfill had contaminated a municipal water supply with trichloroethylene (TCE), tetrachloroethylene (PERC), and other chlorinated solvents.

A 1989 study by the EPA [U.S. Environmental Protection Agency] examined 593 waste sites in 339 U.S. counties, revealing elevated cancers of the bladder, lung, stomach, and rectum in counties with the highest concentration of waste sites.

Increased incidence of leukemia has been reported in a community near a toxic waste dump in North Rhine–Westphalia, Germany.

A 1986 study of children with leukemia in Woburn, Massachusetts, statistically linked the disease to drinking water supplies that had been contaminated by a waste site.

Thus leukemias and bladder cancer are the most commonly reported cancers among populations living near landfills, providing support for the recent findings in New York.

It should come as no surprise that living near a landfill is hazardous to your health—and it doesn't matter whether the landfill holds solid waste or hazardous waste. Hazardous waste landfills hold unwanted toxic residues from manufacturing processes. On the other hand, municipal solid waste landfills hold discarded products, many of which were manufactured from toxic materials. The wastes go out the back door of the factory while the products go out the front door, but after they have been buried in the ground both wastes and products create very similar hazards for the environment, wildlife, and humans. The leachate (liquid) produced inside the two kinds of landfills is chemically identical.

## Low Birth Weight and Small Size

The most commonly reported effect of living near a landfill is low birth weight and small size among children. The first careful study of this subject took place at Love Canal near Niagara Falls, New York. In a blinded study published in 1989, researchers found that children who had lived at least 75% of their lives near Love Canal—the notorious toxic chemical dump—had significantly shorter stature than children who lived farther away from the dump site. These re-

Toles. © 1991 by *The Buffalo News*. Reprinted by permission of Universal Press Syndicate.

sults held up even after controlling for birth weight, socioeconomic status, and parental height.

A previous (1984) study had shown that children who lived near Love Canal had abnormally low weight at birth. The following year, another study confirmed low birth weight in children born to parents living near Love Canal. There does not seem to be any remaining doubt that the children of Love Canal were put in harm's way by exposure to the 20,000 tons of chemical wastes buried in their backyards. Those wastes remain buried there, and the families that have recently moved into homes at Love Canal are likely in danger too.

Studies of children living near other landfills have confirmed these findings. A study of families living near the Lipari landfill in New Jersey reported low birth weight among babies born during 1971–1975, when the landfill was thought to have leaked the greatest quantity of toxic materials into the local environment.

A study of people living near the BKK landfill in Los Angeles County, California, in 1997 reported significantly reduced birth weight among children born during the period of heaviest dumping at the site.

A 1995 study of families living near a large municipal solid waste dump (the Miron Quarry) near Montreal, Quebec, found a 20% increased likelihood of low birth weight among those most heavily exposed to gases from the landfill.

## Birth Defects

At least five studies have reported finding an increased chance of birth defects among babies whose parents live near a landfill. In Wales, the chances of birth defects were doubled among families living near the Nant-y-Gwyddon landfill. A 1990 study in the San Francisco region found a 1.5-fold greater chance of birth defects of the heart and circulatory system among newborns whose parents lived near a solid or hazardous waste site.

A 1990 study of 590 hazardous waste sites in New York state found a 12% increase in birth defects in families living within a mile of a site. A 1997 study of women living within a quarter-mile of a Superfund site showed a two- to four-fold increased chance of having a baby with a neural tube defect, or a heart defect. A preliminary report in 1997 found a statistically significant 33% increased chance of a birth defect occurring in babies born to families living within 3 kilometers (1.9 miles) of any of 21 landfills in 10 European countries.

Researchers at the London School of Hygiene and Tropical Medicine recently reviewed 46 studies of the human health effects of landfills. They concluded, "[L]andfill sites may represent real risks in certain circumstances." They also pointed out that exact mechanism of the hazard remains unknown. Is the biggest hazard air or water pollution? No one knows. But the evidence seems overwhelming: living near a landfill can be dangerous. So long as we remain a society addicted to chlorine chemistry and other toxic technologies, our discards will be toxic, and the places where we bury them will be hazardous to health for a long time to come.

*"With all [the landfill protections] goes a government monitoring process that is a bureaucrat's idea of heaven."*

# Landfills Have Become Safer

Bud Angst

In the following viewpoint, Bud Angst asserts that modern landfills are much safer than town dumps of the past. He describes the advanced technologies—such as multiple liners and collection systems for garbage-produced methane gas—that make modern landfills safe. Angst also contends that ample government oversight prevents abuses that might endanger the health of residents living near landfills. Bud Angst writes for the *Citizen-Standard*, a daily newspaper published in Valley View, Pennsylvania.

As you read, consider the following questions:

1. According to Angst, how thick is a high-density polyethylene liner compared to an average trash bag?
2. What is Bentonite, according to the author?
3. In the author's opinion, why is it unlikely that a landfill's daily records would be faked?

Excerpted from "What Is Inside a Landfill?" by Bud Angst, *Citizen-Standard*, September 9, 1998. Copyright © 1998 by *Citizen-Standard*. Reprinted with permission.

O ld-time municipal dumps and modern landfills are alike in one respect: They both contain a lot of garbage and trash that would otherwise pile up in alleys, backyards, rural roadsides and, in Valley View, Pennsylvania, in abandoned strip mines and quarries. But the similarity ends there.

The town dump of long ago was a smelly, unsightly and unhealthy pile of accumulated and indiscriminately discarded household and industrial rubbish. It was usually located just outside of town, smoldered perpetually, and fed its stinking and poisonous leachate into the nearest creek. And so what? we said then. The creek was polluted anyway. We made jokes about the people downstream in Philadelphia and Baltimore, who were condemned to drinking the water.

## The Modern Landfill: A Layer Cake

The modern landfill presents a strikingly different picture. When operating properly, it stinks, if at all, only where incoming trucks are dumping the day's input. Its input is carefully tracked from birth at some garbage collector's place of business to its eventual graveyard, the landfill. It is buried daily in a complicated protective layer cake with intricacies that boggle the mind. And its leachate is collected through a maze of pipes and valves that resemble a miniature oil refinery.

At the bottom of that protective layer cake is six inches of compacted clay that acts as a subbase for a 60-mil HDPE (high-density polyethylene) secondary liner. 60 mils. Compare that thickness to your ordinary plastic garbage bag which is probably less than 1 mil thick and is by no means made of HDPE, which is tough stuff, virtually impervious to all but the most deliberate break-through attempt.

On top of that secondary liner goes a geonet drainage layer, a screen-like, two-layered insert designed to keep the secondary liner separated from the primary liner, which will come later.

"It keeps like a little breathing space between the two liners," says Mark Harlacker, the man in charge of the Dauphin Meadows Landfill (DML) near Elizabethville, [Pennsylvania] "to allow the flow of liquid." This is, after all, a drainage layer from which the leachate, if any, will be diverted to a treatment plant.

On top of the geonet goes a layer of Bentonite matting. Bentonite comes in pellet or powder form and goes between two sheets of a plastic material. "A lot of times it's used for closing wells," Harlacker says.

When liquid hits it, Bentonite swells to about 300 times its original size. "If something goes down and punctures the primary liner and goes into the Bentonite," says Harlacker, "it will swell the Bentonite and plug the hole."

"It doesn't get hard like concrete," Harlacker explains. "It's almost like a jelly mold, but it's pretty impermeable. It doesn't allow water to go through."

## More Layers

On top of the Bentonite comes another 60-mil liner, the primary liner. Then another geonet drainage layer, topped with geotextile material.

Then comes a foot-and-a-half of "protective cover," essentially the leachate collection system, 18 inches of stone that not only allows collection of the leachate but acts as a buffer between the primary liner and the first load of waste.

---

### What Goes into a Landfill?

In 1990, on average, the solid waste that went into a typical municipal landfill was estimated to contain 38% paper; 18% yard waste (trimmings, leaves, etc.); 8% metals; 7% food; 7% glass; 6% wood; 8% plastics; and 8% miscellaneous. Biodegradable materials may decompose over many years, while non-degradable materials, such as glass and most plastics, remain at the site.

U.S. Environmental Protection Agency, "Solid Waste," http://es.epa.gov, 1998.

---

Finally comes the first load of waste, topped by 6 inches of "daily cover," earth, soil, excavated on site or purchased from some nearby supplier.

Then another layer of waste, typically about 8 feet of it, with its daily layer of cover.

Then begins the process of topping off the "cell," putting the icing on the cake. Topping off starts with an inch of intermediate cover.

"Any area you are out of for 30 days or longer," says Harlacker, "requires an intermediate cover," at least 1 foot of material. Sometimes it's the same material as is used for daily cover, "but more of it," Harlacker points out.

On top of the intermediate cover goes a third layer of HDPE, a 40-mil cap, this time. Then another geonet sandwich (two geotextiles separated by another drainage layer). Then another 1.5 feet of soil cover and then, and only then, the topsoil that will permit the area to grow grass or any grasslike crop.

And then the top layer, the icing, receives its decorative layer of seeds that will eventually turn it into a green mound.

## Controlling Leachate

Throughout the cake are pipes and valves that collect liquids and transport them to a treatment plant presided over by Aaron Maurer, who lives within a stone's throw of the [Dauphin Meadows] landfill and is responsible for seeing to it that the leachate is separated from all heavy metals and other conglomerate that is diverted into safe storage. It is also Aaron's responsibility to see that the liquids are properly decontaminated [and their chemistry aligned with the water of the surrounding environment] before they enter the Wiconisco Creek. The water treatment plant alone is a plumber's delight.

There's also a gas vacuum-operated collection system that channels the garbage-produced methane to a flare that burns it off into the air.

Each of the collection systems are also equipped with failsafe systems that shut down the operation if pre-set limits are exceeded.

With all this goes a government monitoring process that is a bureaucrat's idea of heaven. The Pennsylvania Department of Environmental Protection's Bureau of Solid Waste Management, Bureau of Water Quality, Bureau of Air Quality, and Bureau of Mines all are responsible for checking every landfill. All require meticulously maintained daily records and all can and do make unannounced on-site visits.

Can the daily records be faked? I suppose so. But not forever and not without grave danger of monumental fines or other punishment for the fakers. And the people who keep the records at DML, remember, live in the neighborhood of the place or in nearby communities. If they faked records, they could well be endangering themselves or their relatives. 'Tain't likely.

The Bureau of Solid Waste comes around about twice each month, unannounced. Air Quality, about twice a year except when construction is going on at which time they are constantly underfoot. Water Quality, about once every three months, unannounced, but sometimes oftener. Mining, usually monthly but again, they can and do come oftener. And all of them check the landfill's daily operational reports for their fields of special interest. How quickly do they follow up on citizen complaints? "Usually the same day," Harlacker says, "or the next day."

In light of all this, it's clear there's a big difference between yesteryear's town dumps and today's landfills.

> *"The practice of shipping municipal solid waste thousands of miles from its source . . . has created an 'out of sight, out of mind' culture."*

# Interstate Garbage Shipping Is Harmful

Paul E. Kanjorski

Paul E. Kanjorski is a congressional representative from Pennsylvania. In the following viewpoint, Kanjorski contends that interstate shipping of municipal solid waste threatens the environment and endangers human health. He claims that interstate garbage trucks—many of them unsafe and operated by intoxicated drivers—create pollution and put the lives of other drivers in danger. Kanjorski also argues that when states are freely allowed to ship their garbage to other states, they have no incentive to implement more effective waste management plans, such as recycling programs.

As you read, consider the following questions:

1. According to Kanjorski, how many tons of municipal solid waste did Pennsylvania import in 2000?
2. As stated by the author, what was "Operation Clean Sweep"?
3. What safety problems were found on garbage trucks hauling waste into Pennsylvania in May 2001?

Excerpted from "Perspectives on Interstate and International Shipments of Municipal Solid Waste," by Paul E. Kanjorski, prepared witness testimony before the Subcommittee on Environment and Hazardous Materials, Committee on Energy and Commerce, U.S. House of Representatives, August 1, 2001.

S ince the late 1980s the tonnage of interstate trash imports in several states across the nation has risen dramatically. In response, I have reintroduced legislation that would allow states with comprehensive management plans for the disposal of all waste generated within their own borders to limit the importation of out-of-state trash, and to form voluntary regional compacts with other states to import or export their trash. In fact, this bill, H.R. 667, the Solid Waste Compact Act, was the first bill to address this important issue in the 107th Congress. Additionally, I am an original cosponsor of other legislation we will discuss today, H.R. 1213, the Solid Waste Interstate Transportation Act, and H.R. 1927, the Solid Waste International Transportation Act.*

Total interstate waste shipments continue to increase as older local landfills close and the waste management industry consolidates. My state of Pennsylvania is forced to accept more garbage from other states than any other state in the nation, by far. In 2000, Pennsylvania imported 9.8 million tons of municipal solid waste and 2.5 million tons of other non-hazardous waste from other states, an increase of almost 2 million tons from the 10.4 million tons of out-of-state trash imported the previous year. In 1999, out-of-state trash made up 42.8% of the annual total waste disposal in my state. In 2000, 20 other states reported increased imports of out-of-state trash. Besides Pennsylvania, states such as Virginia, Michigan, Ohio, Indiana, Illinois, Wisconsin, and Oregon share these concerns and each import over a million tons of out-of-state trash annually. Further, New Hampshire, New York, New Jersey, Kentucky, South Carolina, Georgia, and Nevada each import over a half million tons of out-of-state trash annually.

## Protecting the Environment and Human Lives

From my perspective, the legislation offered by my colleagues and me is an attempt to put into action two important ideals that are often talked about in Washington—protecting the environment and promoting local control. It would protect the environment by limiting the current practice of trans-

*At press time, the House of Representatives was still reviewing these bills.

porting garbage hundreds of extra miles from the source, which increases air pollution. It would promote local control by giving states, which already have the duty to ensure that solid waste is disposed of properly, the right to determine whether to accept the waste from other states and nations.

This legislation is all the more crucial in light of the tragic loss of two lives in a recent collision in my district with a truck carrying out-of-state trash. My district includes part of Monroe County, Pennsylvania, where two people were killed in January 2001 on Interstate 80 when a truck carrying out-of-state garbage lost control and crashed into their cars. The driver, who was headed for the Keystone Sanitary Landfill near Scranton, Pennsylvania, walked away with minor injuries and was charged with two counts of homicide by vehicle and two counts of involuntary manslaughter.

---

## Garbage Shipping Is Also Global Injustice

It used to be the poor had the solace of knowing they would only be exploited by the rich of their own country. The wealthy were sons-of-bitches, but they were our sons-of-bitches. Now, globalization has insured that the powerful from any country can abuse the disenfranchised (and increasingly the middle class) from any other country, including the denizens of the American Southwest, almost as easily as sending an e-mail. Like denim jeans and *Playboy*s, oppression has become internationalized and can take many forms, such as garbage, passed around like a rotten pistachio at a party until the luckless at the end of the night eat it.

Christopher Manes, *Northern Lights*, Spring 1999.

---

In May 2001, the Pennsylvania Department of Environmental Protection, the Pennsylvania Department of Transportation and the Pennsylvania State Police launched "Operation Clean Sweep"—surprise trash truck inspections at every landfill, major incinerator, and at checkpoints along the Pennsylvania Turnpike and other interstate highways. What this major enforcement action discovered were hundreds of unsafe trash trucks—86% of the trash trucks had safety and environmental violations and more than one-third were taken off the road. Vehicles hauling waste into Pennsylvania were found to have two of six brakes working, cracked frames, and operating overweight by 30,000 to 40,000 pounds. Additionally, operators were arrested for driving while intoxicated and with suspended licenses. This is a clear sign that far too many trash haulers disregard state safety and environmental regulations, which can lead to accidents like the tragedy on Interstate 80 in January 2000.

## "Out of Sight, Out of Mind"

The practice of shipping municipal solid waste thousands of miles from its source, to be discarded across state and national boundaries, has created an "out of sight, out of mind" culture. Because many communities do not experience the effects of their waste, there is no incentive to implement waste management plans. Efforts to take responsibility for local waste by establishing waste prevention initiatives, recycling programs, and increased landfill and incinerator capacity wane as trash trucks roll out of town. Further, manufacturers lack encouragement to consider the waste management implications of their products. Products continue to be designed and packaged without regard to their volume, toxicity, or recyclability.

Pennsylvania and other states have taken responsibility for waste by increasing recycling and landfill capacity and should be rewarded, not punished, for taking this responsibility. We should work to give states the ability to control the importation of waste so we can protect our environment, promote local control, promote waste management initiatives, and protect the health and safety of our constituents.

*"Restricted borders have no legitimate place
in managing trash or any other product in
our economy. They do not make economic
or environmental sense."*

# Interstate Garbage Shipping Is Beneficial

Bruce Parker

Bruce Parker is executive vice president of the National
Solid Wastes Management Association. In the following
viewpoint, Parker maintains that interstate garbage shipping
helps keep waste disposal costs low by allowing exporting
states to choose the least expensive landfill site for their
waste. For example, New York, which has little available
space for new landfills, saves money by shipping trash to
less-crowded Pennsylvania where landfills are numerous and
tipping fees are low. Parker contends that interstate garbage
shipping also benefits receiving states by generating income
for their waste management facilities.

As you read, consider the following questions:
1. According to Parker, what percentage of the garbage
   disposed of in the United States crosses state borders?
2. What states export the highest percentage of solid waste,
   according to the author?
3. How does the 2001 Congressional Research Service
   report explain the large amount of interstate garbage
   shipping, as stated by the author?

Excerpted from "Perspectives on Interstate and International Shipments of
Municipal Solid Waste," by Bruce Parker, prepared witness testimony before the
Subcommittee on Environment and Hazardous Materials, Committee on Energy
and Commerce, U.S. House of Representatives, August 1, 2001.

I am Bruce Parker, Executive Vice President of the National Solid Wastes Management Association (NSWMA). NSWMA represents private sector companies that collect and process recyclables, own and operate compost facilities and collect and dispose of municipal solid waste. NSWMA members operate in all fifty states.

## The Envy of the World

The solid waste industry is a $43 billion industry that employs more than 350,000 workers. We are proud of the job we do and proud of the contribution our companies and their employees make in protecting the public health and the environment. America has a solid waste management system that is the envy of the world because of our ability to guarantee quick and efficient collection and disposal of trash in a manner that fully conforms with state and Federal waste management laws and regulations.

Our members provide solid waste management services in a heavily regulated and highly competitive business environment. Like all businesses, we are keenly interested in proposals, such as restrictions on the interstate movement of Municipal Solid Waste (MSW), that would change that regulatory or competitive environment, increase the cost of waste disposal and threaten the value of investments and plans we have made in reliance on the existing law. The message I want to leave with you is this: restricted borders have no legitimate place in managing trash or any other product in our economy. They do not make economic or environmental sense. They are contrary to the concept of open borders; contrary to the evolution to bigger, better, more environmentally sound disposal facilities; contrary to our desire to keep disposal costs for taxpayers low, and contrary to the trend toward more innovative, flexible, waste management facilities.

In the balance of this statement, I will share with you our reasons for concern and opposition to H.R. 1213, the "Solid Waste Interstate Transportation Act of 2001", H.R. 1214, the "Municipal Solid Waste Flow Control Act of 2001" and H.R. 1927, the "Solid Waste International Transportation Act of 2001". I will discuss the background and context as we see it, and the flaws in the proposed legislation.*

Interstate waste shipments are a normal part of commerce. In spite of all the impassioned language you have heard from a few states denouncing garbage that moves across state lines, the reality is simple: most states import and export garbage and none are harmed in the process.

According to "Interstate Shipment of Municipal Solid Waste: 2001 Update," which was released by the Congressional Research Service (CRS) in mid-July 2001, 30 million tons of MSW crosses state borders. This equals approximately 13% of the garbage generated in the United States and about 18% of the garbage disposed of in the United States.

These shipments form a complex web of transactions that often involve exchanges between two contiguous states in which each state both exports and imports MSW. In fact, the vast majority of MSW, more than 80%, goes to a disposal facility in a neighboring state. According to the CRS report, 24 states, the District of Columbia and the province of Ontario exported more than 100,000 tons of solid waste in 2000. At the same time, 28 states imported more than 100,000 tons. Fifteen states imported and exported more than 100,000 tons. The CRS report documents interstate movements of MSW involving 49 of the 50 states. Forty-six states, the District of Columbia and one Canadian province export and 42 states import. . . .

Moreover, while some states are the biggest exporters based on tonnage, several small states and the District of Columbia are highly dependent on waste exports. In addition to Washington, DC, which exports all of its MSW, Maryland, New Jersey and Vermont export the highest percentage of solid waste. The reality is that MSW moves across state lines as a normal and necessary part of an environmentally protective and cost effective solid waste management system. Like recyclables, raw materials and finished products, solid waste does not recognize state lines as it moves through commerce.

CRS cites a number of reasons for interstate movements. These include enhanced disposal regulations and the subse-

*At press time, the House of Representatives was still reviewing these bills.

quent decline in facilities. In addition, CRS notes that in larger states "there are sometimes differences in available disposal capacity in different regions with the state. Areas without capacity may be closer to landfills (or may at least find cheaper disposal options) in other states."

## The Role of Regional Landfills

The CRS report notes that the number of landfills in the U.S. declined by 51% between 1993 and 1999 as small landfills closed in response to the increased costs of construction and operation under the Resource Conservation and Recovery Act (RCRA) Subtitle D and state requirements for more stringent environmental protection and financial assurance. The number of landfills in the early 1990s was nearly 10,000 while today there are about 2,600 and the total number continues to decline as small landfills close, and communities in "wastesheds" turn to state-of-the-art regional landfills that provide safe, environmentally protective, affordable disposal.

---

### Trash Highway

A tidal wave of waste has crested on the nation's highways—more than 17 million tons of it shipped annually to out-of-state landfills. In New York alone, trucks loaded with 20 tons of garbage enter the Long Island Expressway every four or five minutes, day and night.

Frank J. Murray, *Insight*, May 12, 1997.

---

Construction and operation of such facilities, of course, requires a substantial financial investment. By necessity, regional landfills have been designed in anticipation of receiving a sufficient volume of waste from the wasteshed, both within and outside the host State, to generate revenues to recoup those costs and provide a reasonable return on investment.

It was widely recognized that the costs to most communities of Subtitle D–compliant "local" landfills were prohibitive. The development of regional landfills was not only entirely consistent with all applicable law, it was viewed and promoted by Federal and State officials and policy as the best solution to the need for economic and environmentally protective disposal of MSW. These regional landfills provide safe and affordable disposal as well as significant contributions to the local economy through host fees, property taxes, and business license fees. Additional contributions to the communities include free waste disposal and recycling services, and in some cases assumption of the costs of closing their substandard local landfills. These revenues and services enable the host communities to improve and maintain infrastructure and public services that would otherwise not be feasible.

## Both the Public and the Private Sectors Oppose Interstate Restrictions

NSWMA is not alone in opposing restrictions on interstate waste. The Solid Waste Association of North America (SWANA), which represents public sector solid waste managers, also opposes these restrictions. At its mid-year meeting in the summer of 2000, SWANA's International Board of Directors voted unanimously to approve a policy statement that supports "the free transboundary movement of solid waste."

Public sector waste managers and private sector waste management companies agree that they can't do their job and protect the public health and the environment while having their hands tied by artificial restrictions based on state lines.

## Host Communities Benefit

MSW also moves across state lines because some communities invite it in. Many communities view waste disposal as just another type of industrial activity, as a source of jobs and income. As noted above, these communities agree to host landfills and in exchange receive benefits, which are often called host community fees, that help build schools, buy fire trucks and police cars, and hire teachers, firemen and policemen and keep the local tax base lower.

## The Broader Context

The proposed legislation before you would radically disrupt and transform the situation I have described. For that reason, as well as the precedential nature of some of the provisions, let me suggest that you consider those bills in a broader context.

The applicability of the Commerce Clause to the disposal of out-of-State waste is well established by a long line of U.S. Supreme Court decisions spanning more than a quarter of a century. As you probably know, the original decision protected Pennsylvania's right to export its garbage to a neighboring state. The Court has consistently invalidated such restrictions in the absence of Federal legislation authorizing them.

Throughout this period, private sector companies did what businesses do: they made plans, invested, wrote contracts, and marketed their products and services in reliance on the rules which clearly protected disposal of out-of-State MSW from restrictions based solely upon its place of origin.

In this fundamental sense, the interstate commerce in waste services is like any other business, and proposed legislation to restrict it should be evaluated in the broader context of how you would view it if its principles and provisions were made applicable to other goods and services, rather than just garbage. Consider, for example, parking lots. Suppose a State or local government sought Federal legislation authorizing it to ban, limit, or charge a differential fee for parking by out-of-State cars at privately owned lots or garages, arguing that they were using spaces needed for in-State cars, and that the congestion they caused was interfering with urban planning, etc. Or suppose they asked for authority to tell privately owned nursing homes or hospitals that they couldn't treat out-of-State patients because of the need to reserve the space, specialized equipment, and skilled personnel to meet the needs of their own citizens. Similar examples can easily be identified—commercial office space for out-of-State businesses, physicians and dentists in private practice treating out-of-State patients, even food or drug stores selling to out-of-State customers.

I would hope that in all of these cases, you would respond to the proponents of such legislation by asking a number of questions before proceeding to support the restrictions: What kind of restrictions do you want? Are they all really necessary? Can you meet your objectives with less damaging and disruptive means? What about existing investments that were made in reliance on the ability to serve out-of-State people? What about contracts that have been executed to provide that service? Would authorizing or imposing such restrictions be an unfunded mandate on the private sector providing those services, or on the public sector outside the State that is relying on them? Would such restrictions result in the diminution of the value of property purchased in reliance on an out-of-State market, and thereby constitute a "taking"? Will the restrictions be workable and predictable? I respectfully suggest that you ask the same questions about the proposed legislation involving restrictions on interstate MSW.

# Periodical Bibliography

The following articles have been selected to supplement the diverse views presented in this chapter.

Ian Avery — "Our Rubbish: Someone Else's Problem?" *International Journal of Human Rights*, Summer 1998.

Mona Chiang — "What a Dump!" *Science World*, April 9, 2001.

Jacques Cousteau, interviewed by Nathan Gardels — "Consumer Society Is the Enemy," *New Perspectives Quarterly*, Spring 1999.

Jean-Michel Cousteau — "We All Live Downstream," *Skin Diver*, November 2000.

Russell Hardin — "Garbage Out, Garbage In," *Social Research*, Spring 1998.

Peter Huber — "Wealth Is Green," www.IntellectualCapital.com, March 23, 2000.

Peter Huber — "Wealth Is Not the Enemy of the Environment," *Vital Speeches of the Day*, April 1, 2000.

Cathy Madison — "Don't Buy These Myths," *Utne Reader*, November/December 1998.

Jim Motavalli — "Zero Waste," *E*, March 2001.

Frank J. Murray — "Load of Rubbish Clogs Interstate," *Insight*, May 12, 1997.

David Pescovitz, ed. — "The Future of Garbage," *Wired*, January 1997.

David Peterson — "Let Them Burn Garbage," *Z Magazine*, April 1996.

William Rathje — "Talking Trash," *Washington Post*, February 15, 1999.

David Schaller — "Our Footprints Are All Over the Place," *Regulatory Intelligence Data*, February 5, 1999.

Robert Steuteville — "The State of Garbage in America," *BioCycle*, April 1996.

U.S. Environmental Protection Agency — "Solid Waste," http://es.epa.gov/oeca/guide/slwast.htm, June 26, 1998.

# Is Recycling Effective?

# Chapter Preface

For environmentalists in China, disposable chopsticks have become a symbol of an increasingly unsustainable way of life. China now uses more than 45 billion pairs of disposable chopsticks every year, which necessitates cutting down 25 million trees. Many experts predict that at the current rate of consumption China will exhaust its remaining forests in about ten years. Chinese truck driver and environmentalist Kang Dahu laments, "Just imagine, years from now, when my grandchildren ask me what happened to all of China's trees, I'll have to say, 'We made them into chopsticks.' Isn't that pitiful?"

Around the world, recycling has become part of the solution to environmental problems such as deforestation. In China, many of those concerned about the environment now carry their own chopsticks, which they wash after every meal and reuse. In the United States, municipal curbside recycling programs grew from 2,700 in 1990 to 8,817 in 1996. Many U.S. corporations have begun using recycled rather than virgin materials to make their products, a shift that, according to many industrial leaders, not only benefits the environment but helps save businesses money. Many environmentalists go so far as to assert that recycling can help transform America's consumeristic lifestyle, which they claim is shallow and unsustainable. Former vice president Al Gore reflects, "In some ways the waste crisis serves as perhaps the best vehicle for asking some hard questions about ourselves. . . . If we have come to see the things we use as disposable, have we similarly transformed the way we think about our fellow human beings?" America's transition to recycling, many believe, is a shift toward a better way of life.

Not everyone agrees that recycling is beneficial, however. John Tierney, a prominent critic of recycling, contends that recycling actually wastes resources. In an article in the *New York Times Magazine*, Tierney argues, "Recycling may be the most wasteful activity in modern America: a waste of time and money, a waste of human and natural resources. . . . There's no reason to make recycling a legal or moral imperative." Critics of recycling claim that it often costs more to manufacture products out of recycled materials than it does to make them from virgin materials. Others maintain that recycling household garbage creates more pollution than simply disposing of it in landfills because additional trucks are required to collect recyclables.

It remains to be seen whether chopstick recycling in China will prevent deforestation or whether garbage recycling in the United States will spark a lifestyle change. Despite questions about its efficacy, however, recycling has become a part of everyday life for many people around the world. The authors in the following chapter debate whether recycling is as necessary, effective, and economical as environmentalists contend.

> "Compared to landfilling, recycling is the economic and environmental favorite by a long shot."

# Recycling Benefits the Environment

Sam Martin

Sam Martin asserts in the following viewpoint that recycling is an effective way to reduce waste. Although recycling programs do adversely impact the environment, Martin contends that alternatives such as landfills—which can pollute the air and water surrounding them—are much more harmful. According to Martin, consumers embrace recycling as a way to help the environment. Sam Martin writes for *Mother Earth News*, a magazine about sustainable living.

As you read, consider the following questions:
1. According to Martin, what impact did the *Mobro 4000* have on America?
2. What specific structural problems are landfills subject to, as stated by the author?
3. In Martin's opinion, why are recycled product sales not what they should be?

To understand the national obsession with saving our garbage we have only to look to the pages of the *Seguin Gazette*, a newspaper in South Texas. "Nothing is junk—save all scrap metal so it can be recycled," a reporter urges. "In multicar families use only one car . . . and take up walking. [Do] your grocery shopping twice a week instead of every day, and if you live close to the market area walk and take your own basket." The story would read like a how-to brochure on environmentally sustainable living in the 21st century—if it weren't an announcement for the War Effort, circa 1942.

During World War II the fact that saving empty toothpaste tubes would keep the country's water and air clean wasn't of imminent concern. Recycling for the war was simple: Save now, have a better world to live in later. Sixty years later, has the message changed so much?

## The Battle of the Bulge

It's no secret that the United States is the most wasteful country on the planet. We dispose of 210 million tons of municipal waste every year, and the yearly costs of that disposal is just shy of $45 billion. Combine residential and business garbage with the truckloads of industrial waste produced in the U.S. and we have an annual pile of trash weighing 12 billion tons. Not surprisingly, what we do with our detritus has become a war of its own.

America's most recent wake-up call to the mess it was making came in 1987, when a trash barge called the Mobro 4000 motored up and down the Eastern seaboard looking for a landfill in which to dump 3,200 tons of New York State's garbage. During thousands of miles of fruitless wandering (the Mobro eventually returned to port, still fully loaded), trash became a headline attraction in newspapers and television stations all over the country.

While waste was news, each story prompted more and more people to question the ethics behind throwing away so much at one time. In 1988, the Environmental Protection Agency (EPA) took the issue seriously enough to recommend that 25% of municipal trash be recycled by the end of a five-year program.

Twelve years of good effort, endless debates and considerable expense have actually made a difference. As of 1995 27% of the country's waste was recycled (compared to 6.3% in 1960), and projected numbers for 2001 report Americans reusing 30% to 35% with recovery rates for paper exceeding 45%.

Nonetheless, what does recycling do for us on a day-to-day basis? It certainly keeps us busy. We set up elaborate sorting systems in our homes—with glass in one bin and paper in the next, rinsing here and bundling there upon penalty of fines or worse: missing the pickup date! And what about the fact that recycling itself is a dirty business, with loud collection trucks plying the predawn streets? It's expensive, as is normal waste disposal, and in increasingly mandatory fashion our taxes are used to pay for an industry that struggles to turn a profit. Is recycling worth it?

Dr. Alan Hershkowitz, director of the National Resources Defense Council, thinks it is. "Everything costs money," he cautions, "including incinerators and landfills." The difference, he explains, is that recycling is designed to ease the impact we have on our environments and alleviate the burden our waste has on our communities. "So yes," Hershkowitz says, "it is worth it."

Since tax money is at the root of any waste solution, the question remains: How can we use the money to deal with our waste most effectively, decrease risks to human health, and foster a healthy environment to live in? It seems that, compared to landfilling, recycling is the economic and environmental favorite by a long shot.

## Closing the Loop on Landfills

If done right, landfills can be a viable disposal option. If done wrong, they can be an environmental and economic disaster.

The main problem with landfills is that they are complicated structures that are difficult to maintain. Of particular concern is the wastewater created inside landfills as leachate. In order to keep the toxic material from leaking into the local drinking water, these football stadium-sized holes require a combination of liners made from clay, high-density polyethylene (HDPE) plastic or composite membranes. But according to the Environmental Research Foundation in Annapolis, Maryland, clay will dry and crack over time, HDPE will degrade with household chemicals, and composite liners made from clay and plastic will leak somewhere between 0.2 and 10 gallons a day after ten years. Even with complex leachate collection plumbing built into landfills, none of these solutions is 100% foolproof (collection pipes tend to clog and back up).

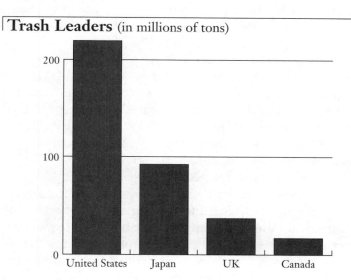

**Trash Leaders** (in millions of tons)

*Mother Earth News,* January 2001.

"The EPA technicians that currently oversee landfill design and regulation have said that their own engineering standards would not last," warns Will Ferretti, executive director of the National Recycling Coalition. "They're saying that they could break down in a 30-year time frame. It's clearly a concern and we have asked the EPA to revisit their regulations in that light."

To be fair, however, recycling doesn't clear every environmental hurdle either. Products remade from recycled waste such as paper and plastic go through a chemical process. In the case of newsprint, there are a dozen or so supposedly nonhazardous chemicals used in the remanufacturing process, including a water/hydrogen peroxide solution to remove ink from the used paper. Paper recycling also uses thousands of gallons of water.

Compared to making paper from virgin materials, however, recycling is clearly more responsible to the environment. In addition to the hundreds of highly toxic chemicals used in papermaking such as chlorine, dioxin and furan, consider what it takes to harvest a forest, build logging roads, and cut and haul trees. The paper recycling industry alone saves 17 trees for every ton of paper it keeps out of the landfill. In 1996 America recovered 42.3 million tons of paper, saving more than 719 million trees.

The plastic manufacturing industry provides an even more compelling case for re-use. According to Hershkowitz, the production of plastics from crude petroleum causes "some of the most substantial public health threats" of any manufacturing process. Indeed, in 1994 U.S. plastic production was responsible for 111 million pounds of toxic air emissions and 12 million pounds of ozone-depleting chemicals.

"You have to ask which activity leaves a smaller footprint on the environment," says Ferretti when comparing recycling to landfilling. "Recycling relies on industrial activity to function, and industrial activity, by nature, has byproducts that can affect the environment. But from a life cycle standpoint, recycling is much more preferable [to landfills] because it has the least impact."

Consequently, the amount of landfills in the U.S. has decreased from 8,000 in 1988 to just over 3,000 in 1996.

## Growing Acceptance

The "reuse and recycle" solution is not a new idea; it has, however, long been recognized as the most economically savvy one. Corporations and big industry such as Ford Motor Co., Herman Miller Furniture and Interface Carpets have been doing it for years because they save millions of dollars by cutting back on production costs. If the numbers don't prove recycling's worth, then common sense does.

"Certainly there is a segment of the population that believes that they have a God-given right to just use stuff up and throw it away," offers Ferretti. "But I don't think that segment of the population will always exist."

The statistics overwhelmingly support his prediction. The most recent EPA statistics (1997) reported that curbside pickup was available in over 49 states and 8,000 cities (Hawaii has since joined the team), and the National Recycling Coalition has estimated that around 84% of the population now has access to a recycling facility. As a result, the amount of municipal waste that has been recycled in the last decade has nearly doubled. By all accounts—public opinion polls and government studies included—people seem to want to recycle.

## Recycling Reduces Pollution

Recycling reduces the risks of air and water pollution from manufacturing processes. Recycling paper cuts air pollution by about 75%. Substituting steel scrap for virgin ore reduces air emissions by 85% and water pollution by 76%.

Department of Environmental Protection, Pennsylvania, *The Benefits of Recycling*, 2001.

Of course, they also have to recycle. Fines and penalties for ignoring recycling laws are stiff, and this Big Brother finger-wagging is part of what prompted John Tierney, a *New York Times* reporter, to write his scathing rebuttal of the whole philosophy in 1996. Entitled "Recycling is Garbage," Tierney's article asserts that the resources, labor and sum personal time involved in recycling far outweigh any environmental or economic benefit. He further suggests that we not only have plenty of landfill space, but that landfills are an economic boon to the communities surrounding them. Tierney's engaging style was an instant hit among anti-recycling political activists, but his often curious interpretation of facts left many scientists puzzled.

"Nothing is perfectly efficient," says Hershkowitz, "and no one I know of is seriously suggesting 100% recovery for recycling. Still, the main roadblock to increased levels of recycling is the absence of a commitment to this issue by industries that have many economic incentives not to recycle or use recycled materials."

Which brings us to a problem in the recycling industry: consumer support. Widely considered the weakest link in the recycling loop, recycled product sales are not what they should be—either because recycled products are more expensive or because they're unavailable. For that reason, the recycling industry isn't getting the financial support it needs to compete with the federally subsidized incentives to which Hershkowitz refers. Most people simply don't realize that they have the option to buy recycled.

"Aluminum, steel and glass are under our noses, and they're not marked like paper usually is," explains George Rutherford of America Recycles Day. "But aluminum, steel and glass have a 30% to 40% recycled content. Plastic doesn't. It's by and large a virgin product. Also, cars are one of the most widely recycled products we have."

Nevertheless, the enormous enthusiasm for recycling programs suggests that there are plenty of reasons to recycle other than being able to buy more stuff, remanufactured or not.

"Recycling is one of those few activities that [allows us] to make a direct connection between our behaviors and some kind of contribution to a quality of life that is hard to find out there," explains Ferretti. "Maybe altruistic is the right word, but I think there's something more innate and more satisfying that is occurring. I would argue that the quality of life both now and for your children and grandchildren is enhanced by that rather modest and mundane action of separating out some portion of our waste and putting it out at the curb for recycling."

While human nature is oftentimes up for speculation, the fact that recycling is the best solution for waste disposal isn't. The evidence and the desire have never been more telling.

## Evidence for the Need to Recycle

Americans receive almost 4 million tons of junk mail a year— 44% is never opened.

Every day, U.S. businesses generate enough paper to circle the earth 20 times. In 1960, Americans disposed of 2.7 pounds of waste per person per day. By 1990, the number had risen to 4.3 pounds per person per day. Every ton of paper recycled saves approximately 17 trees.

Americans throw away 2.5 million plastic bottles every hour.

Five recycled soft drink bottles will make enough fiberfill for a man's ski jacket. 1,050 recycled milk jugs can be made into a six-foot park bench. The United States makes enough plastic film each year to shrink-wrap the state of Texas. If only 10% of Americans bought products with less plastic packaging only 10% of the time, approximately 144 million pounds of plastic could be eliminated from our landfills.

Styrofoam is nonrecyclable. Each year Americans throw away 25 billion Styrofoam cups.

Five hundred years from now, the foam coffee cup you used this morning will be sitting in a landfill. If all morning newspapers read around the country were recycled, 41,000 trees would be saved daily and 6 million tons of waste would never end up in landfills.

| "Recycling is merely an aspirin, alleviating
| a rather large collective hangover."

# Recycling Does Not Solve Environmental Problems

Robert Lilienfeld and William Rathje

Robert Lilienfeld is president of Cygnus Group, a consulting firm working for sustainable development, and editor of the *ULS Report*, a newsletter about conservation and waste reduction. William Rathje is a professor of anthropology at the University of Arizona and coauthor with Cullen Murphy of *Rubbish!* In the following viewpoint, Lilienfeld and Rathje argue that recycling does not solve the world's most serious environmental problems. For example, they claim that recycling does not reduce global warming because it involves processes such as transportation and manufacture that emit greenhouse gases. The authors argue that environmental problems are caused by overconsumption and contend that recycling does nothing to prevent such behavior.

As you read, consider the following questions:
1. According to the authors, what is risk analysis?
2. What is "Parkinson's Law of Garbage," as defined by the authors?
3. In the authors' opinion, why has recycling been the conservation method of choice throughout history?

Excerpted from *Use Less Stuff: Environmental Solutions for Who We Really Are*, by Robert Lilienfeld and William Rathje (New York: Fawcett Books, 1998). Copyright © 1998 by Robert Lilienfeld and William Rathje. Reprinted by permission of the publisher.

While today we admire the majesty of Maya and Sumerian temples—even in ruins—it is also easy to see the engineered disasters that befell the local populations. Both civilizations—the Sumerian [in what is now Iraq] and the Classic Maya [in what is now Mexico]—recycled with gusto. They literally turned old buildings into new. The Sumerians flattened derelict structures to serve as foundations for new structures that were much higher. Sumerian holy words often supported religious observances literally, since broken clay tablets covered with religious texts were regularly used as foundation fill for temples and other structures. When it came to either temples or palaces, the Maya didn't raze a building that was being replaced. Instead, they just added a thick outer shell on top, thereby guaranteeing that the latest temple or palace would be bigger than its predecessors.

## Recycling and Conspicuous Consumption

Both civilizations also recycled daily utensils and tools. The Sumerians had metallurgy and collected and reforged swords, plowshares, and pruning hooks. The Maya often worked broken or chipped stone tools into new shapes that had different uses.

The Maya shared an exquisite irony with the Sumerians before them. All of these ardent recyclers, who reused and recycled tools down to nubbins, never seemed to see the inconsistency in placing hundreds, or even thousands, of totally unused tools in caches to dedicate a building or in the ritual interment of the community's elite. Clearly, both recycling and conspicuous consumption were taken as facts of life that were not to be challenged. Perhaps, in fact, when it came to resource management and conservation, the forest of conspicuous consumption could not be seen through all the twigs and branches of the trees of recycling.

## Have We Learned from the Lessons of the Past?

Few expressions are more familiar or widely accepted than "Those who don't learn from the past are doomed to repeat it." In fact, our society has spent more time and effort than any other on the face of the earth in studying past societies in order to learn about the problems they faced and the missteps they made that led to their downfall.

So what have we learned from all this history that can help us avoid a similar fate? Not that much, we're afraid. Here we are, thousands of years later, passionately recycling, yet consuming with equal gusto!

Once again, we stand on the precipice, poised to make great technological and economic strides, while potentially destroying the environment on which, and from which, all our successes have been built. A look at the potential environmental catastrophes we face can show us why, if we don't stop and rethink our priorities and strategies, the same results might ultimately befall our descendants.

A handful of major issues have been singled out by scientists, environmentalists, policy planners, and the general public as the most serious environmental problems we currently face. These are the problems that seem most likely to lead to a significant degradation, or even collapse, of our late-twentieth-century lifestyles of comfort and convenience, thanks to unwelcome and possibly unforeseen changes in global ecosystems. They are as follows:

- Overpopulation
- Global warming
- Ozone depletion
- Habitat destruction
- Loss of biodiversity
- Depletion of nonrenewable natural resources
- Increased pollution and waste generation

These are huge problems compared to those faced in past societies. What's more, these problems are global, rather than regional or local. Thus, unlike our hunting and gathering ancestors and their nomadic offspring, there's nowhere left for us to run, since geographically speaking, we're already there!

## Preserving the Status Quo

While all these issues are the focus of concern, their current status and the rate of environmental degradation caused by them are the source of major debates. For example, few people would dispute that the effects of global warming would be catastrophic: both the East and West coasts of the

United States would disappear under a flood of water released from melting polar caps, and weather patterns would change, with fertile plains becoming deserts, and deserts fertile plains. Yet many business leaders don't feel there's enough information available to indicate that global warming is occurring, leading them to promote the status quo. The problem with this strategy is—and a few progressive business leaders will admit to this point—if we wait to make sure that the problem exists, when we are finally certain that it does, it will be far too late to do anything to stop it.

Frankly, we find this status quo attitude on the part of modern business leaders to be somewhat surprising, given the current penchant for reengineering and quality management. It's even more confounding when one assesses the situation by applying risk analysis, a favorite quantitative tool in the world of commerce.

Risk analysis looks at two major factors: a.) the degree of risk, and b.) its size or magnitude. A situation with a high degree of risk and a high level of magnitude is obviously a major concern. A situation with a low level of risk and a low magnitude is just the opposite, and a problem with high risk and low magnitude also falls in this "not to worry" category.

It's the last of the four possible scenarios that concerns us: low risk and high magnitude. Most businesspeople tend to shrug off huge environmental concerns because they feel that the risk is low or that it has not yet been demonstrated to be high enough in their minds to warrant attention. And therein lies the problem: *many of the issues we're talking about are so huge that even a small level of probability should be enough to cause careful thought as well as corrective action.*

## Global Issues

In situations involving a whole series of potentially severe problems enmeshed in mountains of debate and disagreement, it would seem logical to find an equal diversity in the number of promoted solutions. Ironically, there is little or no debate over the solution to environmental woes. Virtually everyone's first action of choice is—recycling. Is the recycling response aimed at the target's bull's-eye? Unfortunately, the answer is no. To understand why, we have to take a hard look at what recycling can and cannot do, within the context of solving our large global issues. First, overpopulation. Obviously, no amount of recycling (except for possibly turning latex gloves into condoms) is going to slow the population growth rate. (Too bad we can't take to population control the way we've taken to recycling! Even China, once known for its stringent one-child-per-couple policy, is permitting couples the luxury of a second child.)

What about global warming? Again, with a few hardly significant exceptions, the answer has to be no. The reason is that global warming is caused by one of the things we are not capable of recycling: energy. In fact, recycling may actually contribute to the increase in greenhouse gases and to a decrease in the supply of nonrenewable resources.

You're probably asking yourself, *how is this possible?* Like virtually everything else, recycling involves many processes—collection, transportation, cleaning, manufacture, storage, transport again, and sale—that use energy and generate pollutants just like manufacturing from virgin materials does. The most common denominator, of course, is the gasoline required to move goods around. This is true even when comparing initial procurement of virgin materials with procurement of recyclables, since collecting recyclables means that garbage company trucks now run their routes twice—once for discards and once for recyclables. Thus, the combination of using up nonrenewable resources and the damage caused by pollution can far outweigh the benefits of collecting, re-processing, and transporting recyclables.

## Ozone Depletion

How about ozone depletion? Since it's widely accepted that the ozone hole was largely related to the use of chloroflurocarbons (CFCs) and similar chemical compounds, recycling isn't going to change the picture. In fact, the recycling of CFCs will just produce a continued slow drain into the atmosphere. The best thing to do is what the 1987 Montreal Protocol set out to do: replace these substances with effective, but environmentally benign, substitutes.

What about habitat destruction, loss of biodiversity, and depletion of nonrenewable resources? Recycling can make a difference, but in the long term it will not be enough. This is due to the fact that recycling merely delays the impacts of consumption; it does not decrease them. Recycling does, of course, expand the "use-life" of resources; but eventually they fall out of the recycle-production-consumption cycle, either because they are thrown into the garbage by mistake or carelessness or, more likely, because they degrade after being recycled and cannot be recycled again.

Grimes. © by John Grimes. Reprinted with permission.

Paper, for example, can be recycled, on average, only three times before its fibers are too short and the ink residue too dense to continue to produce a functional recycled product. Recycling will keep each tree's fiber circulating longer; nevertheless, if consumption of paper products continues to increase (and there's no reason to think otherwise), the impact on the environment of cutting trees will also increase. More paper will be recycled, but more paper will also eventually drop out of the system, and more wood fiber will be procured. Thus, recycling will not stop or even simply diminish the various impacts on the environment created by consumption that aggravate global warming (such as emissions from gasoline burned in transportation), or ozone depletion (such as the release of volatile organic compounds [VOCs] in solvents used in industrial cleaning processes), or habitat destruction and loss of biodiversity (such as procuring resources or building new facilities).

OK, but what about increased pollution and waste generation? Recycling must have zeroed in on these problems, and pollution and waste generation are surely decreasing! While it's true that pollution has declined significantly, the changes have far more to do with successful pollution prevention than with recycling. (And as we just stated above, recycling pollutes as well.)

## Parkinson's Law of Garbage

Sadly, the supposition of reduced waste generation is also highly debatable. It is true, of course, that about 27 percent of the materials that would have been discarded are now collected separately for recycling. At the same time, however, we are throwing more and more nonrecyclables away. This is due to a perverse behavior pattern called "Parkinson's Law of Garbage." A derivative of Parkinson's Law, it states: *Garbage will expand to fill the space provided for it.*

Today, many communities have switched to automated garbage collection systems that require standard-size cans of a large size—usually 90-gallon drums. In place of the old standard galvanized-steel 40-gallon cans, the 90-gallon garbage mausoleums provide plenty of space for what was once destined for attics, basements, or storage sheds—such as many items that are considered "household hazardous wastes" (unused paints and pesticides, for example), used materials that might once have been donated to a charitable organization (old clothes, furniture, appliances, and so on), yard wastes that might otherwise have been composted, and even recyclables that might otherwise have been recycled.

The harsh reality is that regardless of recycling rates, we continue to dump at least as much as we have ever dumped—

over 160 million tons annually; global warming continues to be a major threat, thanks to the continued production of huge amounts of carbon dioxide, nitrates, and sulfates; the ozone hole may not still be growing, but even so, it will not be back to its pre-1980 self for another hundred years or so; and "urban flight," combined with our constant creation of, and migration to, the artificially "natural" environments of suburbs, continues to destroy millions of acres of wildlife habitat.

All of this means that, like the residents of Ur and the Classic Maya before us, we have not matched our solutions to the most important problems we currently face.

## Lessons for Us Today

One of the most significant conclusions of archaeology, validated by being taken together with a review of our current environmental status, is that all civilizations—from the earliest to us today—have primarily used recycling as a means to conserve resources and thus cope with their resource management woes and wastes. The disturbing fact is that all earlier civilizations now lie in ruins, and it seems certain that if we follow the path we are on without modification, our remains will soon lie beside them. As a result, it would seem prudent for us to examine two questions raised by the trajectories of ancient societies and our contemporary plight:

1. *Why, at the same time we are recycling, do we feel the need to define success by wasting resources?* This is really not such a difficult question to answer. The behavior of recycling and wasting at the same time is not logical, but it is all too human. We all do it. Have you ever driven miles to a recycling center in a gas-guzzling car to turn in a few cents' worth of newspapers? Or, how about discarding 5 pounds of mail-order catalogs on the same day you place 3 pounds of materials out by the curb in your recycling bin? When we do things like this as individuals, it seems understandable. When we do such things as whole societies, it seems crazy—but still all too human.

2. *Why has recycling been the conservation method of choice throughout history?* The most obvious reason is that people did not see the big picture clearly enough to determine

where the most critical threat lay. Thus, the government of Ur did not comprehend their environmental degradation and resource waste problems and consequenty followed policies that not only did not cure the difficulties but served to exacerbate them. The Classic Maya, as well, seem not only to have missed seeing the need to compete in trade by investing manpower and resources into new techniques and product designs, but also invested their available manpower and other resources primarily in nonproductive forms of warfare and conspicuous consumption.

Similarly today, we recycle with gusto as we discard 20 million tons of food a year, offer "no annual fee" credit cards to teenagers, and barrage homeowners to remortgage their houses in order to consume more things that will eventually become waste. Thus, although separated by vast gulfs of time and geography, each of these societies didn't—or don't—see their most pressing problems, concentrating instead on recycling and material displays of success—an illogical but familiar human foible.

So, finally, what is the real issue we must face?

## It's Consumption, Pure and Simple!

The simple truth is that *all* of our major environmental concerns are either caused by, or contribute to, the ever-increasing consumption of goods and services. But rather than deal with the effects of too much shopping and purchasing, we've taken the time-honored path of shooting the messengers— the packaging, dirty disposable diapers, foam cups, and other discards that are signs of consumption but are not really consumption itself. And in so doing, we have focused only on the symptoms—too much waste and pollution—and not the underlying problem itself.

In this context, recycling is merely an aspirin, alleviating a rather large collective hangover. But just as aspirin does not prevent hangovers, recycling will not prevent overconsumption. In fact, by putting too much faith in recycling, we are actually rewarding ourselves for overconsuming. Think about it. We feel good when we fill the recycling bin. In reality, we should feel good when there's no waste to put in it at all!

*"Recycling has proven to be the greatest jobs producer of any waste management option."*

# Recycling Is Economical

Allen Hershkowitz

Allen Hershkowitz is a senior scientist with the National Resources Defense Council, an environmentalist organization. In the following viewpoint, Hershkowitz argues that taking into account the environmental, social, and health costs associated with landfilling and incinerating garbage, recycling is a more economical waste disposal option. According to Hershkowitz, recycling benefits local economies by creating jobs and improving property values. In contrast, he claims that landfills hurt communities because the odors and pollution they produce discourage capital investment and lower the socioeconomic status of the community.

As you read, consider the following questions:

1. What costs does the EPA claim must be considered in order to assess the cost-effectiveness of recycling, as related by Hershkowitz?
2. As quoted by the author, what landfill problems does the EPA claim can result in property damage?
3. How has New York City benefited from the operation of recycling manufacturing plants, according to Hershkowitz?

O pponents of recycling claim that shipping wastes to a landfill is economical. But as of 1995, the costs for landfilling wastes in the United States—not including collection, processing, and transport—varied by more than 300 percent, depending on the region and the technology employed at the facility. To officials in charge of municipal waste management programs, it is a well-known fact that the cost of any integrated municipal solid waste management program, especially those as extensive and complicated as the ones serving many of America's largest cities, is always variable. Among the reasons for this: landfill tipping fees [which are fees charged for using the landfill] vary widely, capital and operating budgets change annually, waste collection and hauling services are highly competitive and prices for them change often, and the value of recovered materials also fluctuates. Thus, it is impossible to claim, as the antirecycling interests do, that relying on a landfill is—and always will be—the cheapest waste management option.

## Landfills: Not So Cheap After All

It is complicated to establish financial accounting equivalents for the dissimilar costs and benefits recycling and landfilling engender. Despite claims that recycling is not cost-competitive when compared with landfilling, in fact no full life-cycle-cost accounting protocol that conforms with generally acceptable accounting principles has been established that convincingly monetizes and compares these dissimilar costs and benefits. Sometimes advantages accrue at the local level that benefit recycling; sometimes the revenue from recycling is less cost-competitive. As the Environmental Protection Agency (EPA) has recently observed, none of this undermines the larger strategic value of recycling:

> Full Cost Accounting (FCA) helps decision makers . . . by providing complete cost information, including direct and indirect costs as well as past and future expenses. Instead of looking at all of these costs, some solid waste managers have simply counted the costs associated with collecting and processing recyclables when comparing recycling to alternative methods of waste management. It's no wonder that antirecyclers can argue that curbside recycling doesn't pay. This equation leaves out the revenues from selling secondary ma-

terials and reductions in landfilling or incineration costs. . . . However, current FCA systems do not take into account broader environmental, health and social costs. While these costs cannot be easily measured or readily valued, they are important and we must begin to quantify them so that we can demonstrate that recycling is not garbage. We can start by reframing the discussion from an emphasis on the local costs of collection and landfill tipping fees to an examination of all of the costs and benefits of waste management policies, on a national and even global basis.

In fact, tipping fees at landfills have been increasing at more than twice the rate of inflation every year since 1986 in virtually every region of the United States (overall they increased by 300 percent since that time), and they are expected to continue to rise 7 percent per year (more than double the projected rate of inflation) for the foreseeable future. At the same time that tipping fees at landfills have been increasing dramatically, the rate of recycling has almost tripled. Without waste disposal pressure being relieved by an almost 24 percent recycling rate, which diverts about 42 million tons of municipal waste from landfills and incinerators annually, the inflationary climb of landfill tipping fees would be even steeper.

## Community Economic Development: Recycling Versus Landfills

With their perspective on environmental policies principally driven by economic arguments, it is not surprising that the antirecycling voices offer economic development and jobs production as a consequent benefit of landfill-dependent solid waste management strategies. Glorifying a landfill development in Charles City County, Virginia, the Reason Foundation [a national research and education organization] observed:

> In exchange for a host benefit fee of at least $1.1 million per year, Charles City County, Virginia, accepted a regional landfill. Thanks to the landfill, the county cut property taxes by 20 percent, even though spending on schools went up.

[Journalist] John Tierney, who lifted the Reason Foundation's reference to the Charles City County landfill to the pages of the *New York Times Magazine* [in his article, "Recycling Is Garbage" stated:

The landfill's private operator . . . pays Charles City County fees totaling $3 million a year—as much as the county takes in from all its property taxes. The landfill has created jobs. . . . [P]oliticians in other states [who] have threatened to stop the importing of New York's garbage would only be depriving their own constituents of jobs and tax revenue.

## The Facts

Far from strengthening local economies and producing jobs, landfills actually produce very few jobs, the least of any waste management option, and a review by the EPA of the socioeconomic impact of landfills concludes they hurt established local economies. Also, the jobs produced by landfills involve exposure to many workplace and environmental hazards. By contrast, recycling has proven to be the greatest jobs producer of any waste management option, and many of the most prosperous communities in the United States have the best organized recycling programs.

According to the EPA, landfills reduce the value of property around them:

> Various [adverse] welfare effects may be associated with [landfills]. . . . Studies indicate that unpleasant odors can discourage capital investment and lower the socioeconomic status of an area. [Landfill] odors have been shown to interfere with daily activities, discourage facility use, tax revenues and payrolls. . . . [In addition to adverse health effects] the associated property damage [caused by landfill gases, fires, and explosions] is a welfare effect. Furthermore, when the migration of methane and the ensuing hazard are identified, adjacent property values can be adversely affected.

Mention the community's recycling program to a prospective home buyer and the response is likely to be an appreciative nod. Mention that the community hosts a regional landfill and the prospective buyer is likely to look elsewhere.

The utopian vision of simple, cheap, and environmentally safe landfills helping to finance schools and libraries is an exceptionally rare phenomenon and logically inconsistent. It is precisely because of the documented adverse environmental, economic, and public health threats caused by landfills that so few communities want them. It is for these reasons that developers of landfills have had to pay for community benefits such as schools and computers to those very few and very poor (and often minority) communities forced to consider landfilling as an economic-development option.

---

## Incalculable Costs

What's really being wasted in America is the well-being of the next generation and those that follow. By crassly consuming resources and leaving behind waste, we're dumping the cost of restoration on them. The measure of our humanity is the degree to which we conserve Earth's bounties for those who follow in our footsteps, while sparing them the burden of cleaning up our messes.

*ReThink Paper*, 1996, www.rethinkpaper.org.

---

For-profit or government-run recycling facilities produce more jobs than for-profit or government-run landfills. As business ventures, both types of facilities are profitable, so why not promote the process that produces more jobs and helps reduce pollution at manufacturing plants? For example, the Charles City County, Virginia, landfill cited by the Reason Foundation, and later in "Recycling Is Garbage," employs approximately 55 people and is designed to manage approximately 6,000 tons of waste per day, or one job for every 34,000 tons of waste managed annually. (Predictably, the Charles City landfill is in a poor community that is 62 percent minority.) When paper, plastics, metals, and other materials are deposited at that landfill, they become unavailable for productive use more or less forever.

## Recycling Success

By contrast, New York City's Bronx Community Paper Company, a recycled newsprint mill that was initiated by NRDC and a local community group, will produce 600 permanent jobs for a recycling project (including wastepaper processing) that will remanufacture almost 900 tons of wastepaper a day into newsprint, or one job for every 459 tons of waste managed annually. And far from desecrating a rural greenway, as the developers of the Charles City County landfill did, this mill will clean up and bring economic activity and jobs back to an industrial site abandoned for a quarter of a century. Similarly, the Visy paper recycling mill under construction in New York City in Staten Island, which will also redevelop an abandoned industrial site and process approximately 900 tons per day of wastepaper, anticipates 200 full-time jobs, or one job for every 1,375 tons of waste handled each year. Thus, the two recycling mills under development in New York City could produce anywhere between twenty-four and seventy-four times more jobs per ton of waste handled than would shipping the same amount of material to the Charles City County landfill or any other landfill. And rather than being located at landfills far removed from New York City, the jobs produced by recycling manufacturing plants there are local, so the city will realize economic multiplier benefits in the form of tax revenue, raised family income, and ancillary business activity. According to analysts at the New York City Economic Development Corporation, these latter multiplier benefits will add millions of dollars in additional benefits to the city's economy. (None of the job estimates include construction jobs. More construction jobs are produced in developing a manufacturing plant for recycling than are produced when land is excavated to develop a landfill. In New York City more than 4,000 construction jobs for two years will be necessary to build the recycled paper mills.) Nor is New York City's situation unique. Studies prepared in dozens of states have confirmed that recycling is a better stimulator of jobs and economic development than is landfilling and incineration. For example, one recent study prepared by the Texas Natural Resources Conservation Commission found that "Recycling added about 18.5 *billion* in value to the economies of 12 Southern states and Puerto Rico in 1995."

*"Recycling is supposed to 'save' resources, but when the full range of resources is considered, it may instead waste resources."*

# Current Recycling Programs Are Too Expensive

Clark Wiseman

In the following viewpoint, Clark Wiseman contends that recycling is expensive because it is done excessively. He claims that recycling involves higher costs than does land-filling because more trucks are needed for collection. According to Wiseman, landfills are a better method of waste disposal because they are safe, cost-effective, and space is plentiful. Clark Wiseman is associate professor of economics at Gonzaga University.

As you read, consider the following questions:
1. In Wiseman's opinion, why have landfill costs risen?
2. How much per ton did the recycling cost of Seattle's program exceed the avoided disposal cost, according to the author?
3. As stated by Wiseman, how much space would be required to landfill one thousand years' worth of trash produced by the United States?

From "Advocates Tout Flawed Study, Misconceptions," by Clark Wiseman, *San Diego Union-Tribune*, September 21, 1997. Copyright © 1997 by Union-Tribune Publishing Company. Reprinted with permission.

No reasonable person would disagree with the Natural Resources Defense Council's (NRDC) position that recycling is desirable. Recycling has been carried out on a massive scale throughout human history, and undoubtedly dates from prehistoric times, when implements and animal skins were first modified and converted from one use to another. Hence, in a broad sense, recycling indeed has a "proven record."

## Appropriate Levels of Recycling

The real issue is the appropriate level of recycling. The NRDC report refers to "a small but vocal chorus of anti-environmental interests" who "have tried to cast doubt on the value of recycling."

This chorus is actually composed of those who favor the most efficient level of recycling. In contrast, the NRDC appears to believe that we should recycle as much as possible.

The NRDC report as a whole suffers from its fundamentally anecdotal, emotive approach to a topic that deserves a more detached and analytical assessment. Much of the report is devoted to a broadside condemnation of any and all use of virgin materials.

To refute these claims would require a report as long as NRDC's 86 pages. Instead, I will address the main issue, the costs of recycling. All economic costs are due to resource use—ultimately the use of human resources and natural resources. When we say that one management option is more costly than another we are saying that it uses more resources than the other. Recycling is supposed to "save" resources, but when the full range of resources is considered, it may instead waste resources. [Journalist] John Tierney's article [in the *New York Times* entitled "Recycling Is Garbage"] on recycling concluded that it does.

If many of the 7,000 curbside collection programs now being operated or subsidized by local municipalities are more costly than the major alternative, landfilling, then we must conclude that this level of recycling is excessive.

The NRDC report fails to provide any relevant and meaningful evidence to show that recycling costs the same as or less than landfilling. It cites the recent increasing costs of landfilling as a justification for more recycling, but fails to note the cause of the increase. The higher environmental standards that landfills must meet, not a shortage of landfill capacity, are pushing up costs. Landfill capacity has actually increased, as the report concedes.

The net cost of a recycling program is the cost of the program minus whatever is earned from selling recyclables. If recycling saves resources, this net cost will be less than the cost of the landfilling that has been avoided. But this is not typically the case.

To illustrate with a real world example consider a study of recycling in the state of Washington. A study prepared for Clean Washington Center, a division of Washington's Department of Community, Trade, and Economic Development, reported that per-ton recycling costs were less than disposal costs for each of four Washington programs: Seattle, Spokane, Vancouver, and Bellingham.

---

## Recycling Failures

Recycling programs as popularly conceived are usually failures. The evidence ranges from the piles of collected metals left unused after World War II to the mounts of unwanted glass that pile up in recycling centers today. There simply isn't a big enough market for the deluge of recovered residuals such programs generate. Often they collect materials whose value is less than the cost of collection alone, making "recycling" more wasteful than simple disposal.

Jesse Walker and Pierre Desrochers, *American Enterprise*, January/February 1999.

---

Even if one accepts the study's cost figures at face value, the study made a fundamental and common mistake. It assumed that recycling results in lower disposal collection costs. However, recycling does not avoid disposal collection costs. It adds to them. Trucks must still make the same number of stops and cover the same routes—but this time it is additional trucks.

No one (not even the NRDC) thinks that recycling will completely replace landfilling. Collection costs are fixed costs, and they are the largest component of disposal costs—historically about two-thirds of the total waste management bill. The study compared the cost of recycling a ton of material with the cost of disposing of it in a landfill, but failed to acknowledge that recycling means additional collection by additional trucks. When this is recognized, the conclusion is reversed.

In every case studied by the Clean Washington Center, including Seattle's highly vaunted program, the net recycling cost exceeds the avoided disposal cost by between $15 and $90 per ton.

Furthermore, these figures assume that all municipal recycling represents a diversion of material that would have gone into landfills. Yet some material would have been recycled anyway—the convenience of curbside pickup simply diverts it from private recycling to municipal recycling. Thus, the study overstates the amount of recycling actually achieved.

## Exaggerating the Problems of Landfills

In addition to distorting the cost of recycling, the NRDC report vastly overstates the problems of landfills. The report dwells on the horrors of antiquated landfills, presenting them as current practice. It does not mention the modern ones that comply with the current stringent landfill regulations.

It also suggests that we are running out of landfill space. But let us suppose that all the municipal trash produced in the United States in one year were put into one landfill to a depth of 100 yards (which is less than the depth of the Fresh Kills landfill in Staten Island [in New York City]). All this trash would require a pit two-thirds of a square mile on each side. If we were to collect 1,000 years' trash in the same place, we would need an area 30 miles square. If there is a waste disposal problem, it does not relate to the gross space requirements of landfilling.

Furthermore, NRDC's emphasis on landfill closures is disingenuous. The great majority of landfills are small and designed for only about ten years of operation, so that about half of them close in every five-year period. The relevant consideration is new landfill capacity, rather than the number. One reason capacity is increasing is that most new landfills are large.

Nor does recycling of wastepaper necessarily save trees.

The notion that recycling is protecting stately old trees is erroneous; large trees are more valuable for lumber or plywood than for paper production.

In sum, the NRDC doesn't have much of a case when it pushes for ever more recycling. Its lack of objectivity may even undermine its credibility with all but the most unquestioning of recycling enthusiasts.

> *"It is time for an environmental reformation, in which lawmakers change public policy to reflect the wastefulness of recycling."*

# Mandatory Recycling Wastes Resources

Doug Bandow

Doug Bandow maintains in the following viewpoint that mandatory recycling programs are expensive and wasteful. Moreover, he contends that recycling is unnecessary because natural resources and sites to dispose of garbage are plentiful. Bandow argues that industry—which pays the greatest recycling costs—should pressure the federal government to eliminate mandatory recycling. Doug Bandow is a senior fellow at the Cato Institute, a libertarian public policy research foundation.

As you read, consider the following questions:
1. How does Bandow explain the moral fervor behind recycling?
2. According to the author, how much more does it cost New York City to collect recyclables than it would cost to bury them?
3. What recycling regulations have resulted from industry's failure to confront the government about the wastefulness of recycling, as stated by Bandow?

Excerpted from "Our Widespread Faith in Recycling Is Misplaced," by Doug Bandow, *This Just In*, August 27, 1997. Copyright © 1997 by Copley News Service. Reprinted with permission.

The Earth. It's hard not to like it. Many people adore it. Indeed, there has long been a strand of environmentalism that treats nature as divine. So-called Deep Ecologists, for instance, term their "eco-terrorist" attacks acts of worship to the planet. Few Americans would go so far, of course, but many of them worship in their own way. They recycle.

## The Price of Moral Fervor

In 1997 a wandering garbage barge [called the *Mobro 4000*, which could not find a place to dump its load] set off a political crisis: Where will we put our trash? The media inflamed people's fears of mounting piles of garbage. A variety of interest groups—particularly "public relations consultants, environmental organizations, waste-handling corporations," according to journalist John Tierney—lobbied to line their pockets. Politicians seeking to win votes enacted a spate of laws and regulations to encourage and often mandate recycling.

But while politics did help create an industry, it did not generate the moral fervor behind it. Many people see recycling as their way to help preserve the planet. For some, it may be the environmental equivalent of serving time in Purgatory, attempting to atone for the materialist excesses of a consumer society. It allows one to feel good about oneself even while enjoying every modern convenience.

This moral fervor comes at a price. A new study from the Reason Foundation, "Packaging, Recycling, and Solid Waste," concludes that recycling, though sometimes beneficial, all too often wastes resources. But then, it has long been known that most trash isn't worth reusing, recycling programs usually lose money, and landfills offer a safe disposal method.

Indeed, in 1996 [*New York Times* journalist] John Tierney wrote a devastating article for *The New York Times Magazine* titled "Recycling is Garbage." He declared that the emperor had no clothes: "Recycling may be the most wasteful activity in modern America: a waste of time and money, a waste of human and natural resources."

His points were many. For instance, packaging saves resources, reducing food spoilage. Fast-food meals generate less trash per person than do home-cooked meals. The cheapest way to dispose of garbage is in a landfill. Modern dumps incorporate a range of safeguards and take up a minuscule amount of space.

## No Reason to Recycle

A. Clark Wiseman of Spokane's Gonzaga University figures that, at the current rate, Americans could put all of the trash generated over the next 1,000 years into a landfill 100 yards high and 35 miles square. Or dig a similar-size hole and plant grass on top after it was filled.

---

### Competition Is Best

Market-driven competition is the best way to [conserve resources and protect the environment]. That is because the price of each option represents its cost to society: the value of the water, energy, land, labor, and other resources the disposal option requires. Hence, by allowing competition between disposal options, we enable the most resource-efficient (the least expensive) option to win in any given case. Yet state and local governments don't follow this advice. They try to manage their waste the same way the formerly communist nations tried to manage their entire economies. The result is wasted resources.

Competitive Enterprise Institute, *Environmental Briefing Book*, March 1, 1999.

---

Recycling, in contrast, costs money. New York City's mandatory program spends $200 more per ton to collect recyclables than it would cost to bury them, and another $40 per ton to pay a company to process them. Tierney figures the value of the private labor wasted complying with the rules (rinsing, taking off labels, sorting) to be literally hundreds of dollars more per ton.

Yet there is no environmental reason to recycle trash. Resources are not scarce. In fact, much newsprint comes from trees grown for that specific purpose. Even Worldwatch, a reliably hysterical [environmental] group that has constantly (though luckily, so far inaccurately) predicted impending environmental doom, now acknowledges: "The question of scarcity may never have been the most important one."

Moreover, making recyclables generates waste. For instance, producing paperboard burger containers yields more air and water pollution and consumes more energy than does manufacturing polystyrene clamshells. It takes more water to recycle newsprint than to make it afresh.

## Environmental Reformation

How can such a wasteful practice persist? Tierney concluded: "By turning garbage into a political issue, environmentalists have created jobs for themselves as lawyers, lobbyists, researchers, educators and moral guardians. Environmentalists may genuinely believe they're helping the Earth, but they have been hurting the common good while profiting personally."

Tierney's article infuriated environmentalists, but was ignored by business, which is paying much of the cost of the recycling liturgy. Only silence emanated from companies that have the most to gain from returning garbage to the marketplace.

Yet inaction is a prescription for more regulation. The federal government is considering increasing its national objective for recycling from 25 percent to 35 percent, 41 states already impose some form of goal or mandate regarding trash reduction and recycling, and some jurisdictions are considering new laws, such as so-called advance disposal fees. Politicians who care little about facts and feel political pressure only from environmentalists are likely to add new rules and toughen existing ones.

If people want to worship the Earth by recycling, they are certainly free to do so. But the government shouldn't dragoon skeptics into the same wasteful ceremonies. It is time for an environmental reformation, in which lawmakers change public policy to reflect the wastefulness of recycling.

| "*Mandatory recycling is the only option for conserving and reusing finite resources.*"

# Mandatory Recycling Programs Work

William J. Cohen

In the following viewpoint, William J. Cohen argues that mandatory recycling programs are an effective way to conserve resources and reduce waste and pollution. Cohen describes the success of the mandatory recycling program in Lunenburg County, Nova Scotia, Canada, where a single recycling center efficiently processes household garbage—which residents have willingly separated—for resale. According to Cohen, the program has succeeded in diverting 60 to 70 percent of the county's waste from area landfills. William Cohen is a city and regional planning consultant.

As you read, consider the following questions:
1. As stated by Cohen, why did Lunenburg County decide to implement a mandatory recycling program?
2. How are separations done in Lunenburg County, according to Cohen?
3. According to the author, what is recycled compost used for?

From "Recycle or Else," by William J. Cohen, *Planning*, December 2000.
Copyright © 2000 by American Planning Association. Reprinted with permission.

W hat a wonderful way to spend a summer vacation—
visit paradise and tour a recycling plant.

This, in a nutshell, is the lasting impression and experience I would have on my first trip to Nova Scotia, Canada's picturesque maritime province.

## Mandatory Recycling

Flying into Halifax, Nova Scotia, from Philadelphia on a warm summer afternoon and then driving for an hour and a half to stay with some old friends in Petite Riviere on Nova Scotia's Atlantic coast, I was looking forward to a week of complete change, lush scenery, expansive beaches, and learning something about the people.

Well, my first experience about the people was to be informed by one of my hosts, Priscilla Thompson, who said, "We have mandatory recycling here; but you don't have to do it." I immediately responded that by all means, "I will do what you do." In fact, I was to become a participant-observer in a recycling program that has become an accepted way of life in Nova Scotia. I was so impressed with its simplicity and efficiency that my friends arranged a personal guided tour of the recycling plant.

For the next week, as I took up residence in my own cottage, I quickly learned the dos and don'ts of recycling in this Canadian province. While I was accustomed to voluntary recycling in my home town of Wilmington, Delaware, what was unique about my summer experience is that recycling in this corner of Canada is required; it has public support; it is efficient and cost effective; and it works.

## What I Learned

Based on this experience, my firm belief is that mandatory recycling is the only option for conserving and reusing finite resources. This may be the only way to maintain a way of life that relies so heavily on consumption.

The recycling program I observed is run by Lunenburg County, which includes four municipalities with a total population of slightly more than 38,000. In 1991 the four municipal councils in the region, including Lunenburg County and the towns of Bridgewater, Lunenburg, and Mahone Bay, approved a regional recycling strategy that would offer an alternative to the county's system of burning and landfilling, a system on a collision course with Nova Scotia's clean air goals. Those clean air goals were to be met by 1996, and the province's waste reduction goals were to be met by 2000.

Nova Scotia is unique among Canadian provinces in having established a provincewide mandatory recycling program. It is also the first province to achieve the national goal of reducing the volume of waste sent to landfills by at least 50 percent.

Lunenburg County's strategy was fairly direct: It would include the operation of a separation plant for recyclables, a composting plant for both source-separated organic garbage and mixed waste, and a dry landfill for the residue. Hazardous wastes and large discarded items, such as appliances, also would be recycled. The strategy's guiding principle was source separation.

Individual households are the prime generator of solid waste. After conducting a six-month pilot study of 1,000 households in 1992 and 1993, the county reported that one-third of all solid waste was diverted from the landfill. Moreover, 84 percent of the study participants liked the program. With these results, the county decided to push ahead with a mandatory, countywide recycling system.

## Making Source Separation Work

Each household separates four "streams" of waste which are then deposited in their own containers and placed at the curb or roadside and collected every two weeks. A brochure on the refrigerator in my cottage served as a constant reminder about what kind of waste goes where. Here is how the separations are done in Lunenburg County:

• Recyclable containers go in a blue bag. Includes all household plastic, metal, glass containers, and cartons.

• Recyclable paper goes in a grocery bag. Includes all newspapers, office paper, junk mail, books, and cardboard boxes.

• Organics go into a green cart. Includes food, kitchen scraps, meat and fish bones, and soiled, waxed, and wet paper.

• Everything else goes in an acceptable bag. Includes all other waste except hazardous waste. Because the four streams of waste are collected every two weeks, an obvious question came to mind: "What would happen if I don't separate, and just leave everything at curbside in one container?" My friend Ames Thompson responded: "It simply won't be picked up!"

I was to learn that the municipal collection people give everything a quick inspection to make sure that the waste has been separated correctly before they pick it up. If, for example, they find a blue bag that contains an nonrecyclable item, they slap on a bright red sticker marked "rejected." Property owners then have two options: Either reseparate or haul the garbage to the recycling center—for a fee. In either case, the solid waste must ultimately be separated before it is deposited in the collection trucks, the recycling facility, or the landfill.

## At the Recycling Center

The recycling—or processing—center is where the source-separated waste is sorted and composted. Processing involves four functions: the separation and sorting equipment for the dry recyclables such as the cans, bottles, and plastics found in the blue bag; the sorting and baling of various paper products in the grocery bag, as well as corrugated cardboard from residential and nonresidential sources; the processing equipment for incoming organics from the green cart; and mixed waste processing. At the recycling center each waste stream is handled and processed separately.

The blue bags are loaded onto a conveyor and broken open by hand. A magnetized cross conveyor handles the steel food cans. The material then passes over a shaker screen so that any small debris and broken glass can be removed. Next, aluminum cans and plastic bottles are separated and glass containers are color separated.

Mixed paper travels by conveyor past sorting stations, where various grades are sorted out by hand. Corrugated cardboard bypasses most of the sorting, except when contaminants are removed, and is sent directly to the baler. All of the sorted recyclable containers and paper materials are stored in bunkers or bins until there is enough for baling and shipment to various buyers.

All of the household organics—lawn trimmings, meat and

## The Growth in Recycling Is Leveling Off

Percentage of trash that is:

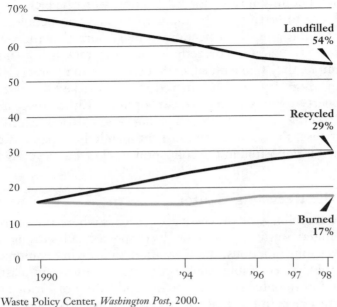

Waste Policy Center, *Washington Post*, 2000.

fish bones, kitchen scraps, along with soiled and wet paper products, as well as boxboard and organics from businesses—are diverted for composting in a "source-separated vessel." Organics are dumped onto a tipping floor and transferred by conveyor past a visual inspection station. There contaminants are removed. The material then passes through a shredder and onto a trommel screen (or sieve) that further breaks down the organic material. Most of the organic material will pass through the smaller two-inch holes of the trommel screen on its way to composting.

The remaining refuse goes through a separate inspection, similar to the recyclables, to remove bulky items or contaminants. Source separated organics and mixed waste are always processed separately, using the same equipment but avoiding cross contamination. Materials are kept separate during the composting phase.

Richard Wilson, Lunenburg's recycling coordinator, was

eager to point out how recycled materials can be reused. One of the most impressive processes was the composting of the organic and mixed waste. That waste is paddle-turned through a composting vessel that constantly mixes, aerates, and waters the material, which moves about eight to 10 feet per day over the course of a three-week maturing period. As the microorganisms flourish inside the moving material, the heat generated there destroys any harmful bacteria, and the air pumped into the vessel eventually gets exhausted outside of the building to prevent an odor buildup.

After three weeks the organic material is screened for items that failed to break down, and is stockpiled outside for its final curing process. Several weeks must pass before the compost is ready for market, typically for farming, horticultural, and garden use.

## Capture Rates

By the late 1990s Lunenburg's recycling program claimed the overall residential landfill diversion rate had reached 67 percent, which means that 80 percent of the county's households were source-separating 80 percent of their waste correctly.

Wilson says that waste collected from homes and small businesses during fiscal 1999–2000 achieved a 60 to 70 percent diversion rate. This was well above the 50 percent diversion target set by the province of Nova Scotia for the year 2000.

If we are serious about conserving and reusing our finite resources, American communities should study Lunenburg's successful recycling program closely.

# Periodical Bibliography

The following articles have been selected to supplement the diverse views presented in this chapter.

| | |
|---|---|
| *American Prospect* | "Garbage In, Garbage Out," September 10, 2001. |
| David Bacon | "Recycling—Not Always Green to Its Neighbors," *Neighborhood Works*, May/June 1998. |
| William Bruck | "Making Recycling an Integral Part of the Economy of the Future," *OECD Observer*, Summer 2000. |
| Richard A. Denison and John F. Ruston | "Recycling Is Not Garbage," *Technology Review*, October 1997. |
| Christopher Douglass | "Government's Hand in the Recycling Market: A New Decade," *Policy Study Number 148*, Center for the Study of American Business, September 1998. |
| *Economist* | "America's Recyclers: A Funny Sort of Market," October 18, 1997. |
| Fred Friedman | "Creating Markets for Recycling," *Dollars and Sense*, July/August 1999. |
| Eric Lombardi | "Beyond Recycling—Zero Waste or Darn Near," *BioCycle*, September 2001. |
| Shari Missman Miller | "Talking Trash: Recycling at Work," *OfficeSolutions*, March 2001. |
| Lynn Scarlett | "Recycling Is Politically Correct but Not Always Environmentally Friendly," *San Diego Union-Tribune*, October 6, 1999. |
| Daniel Scott | "Redeeming the Blue Box," *Alternatives Journal*, Fall 1999. |
| Dan Seligman | "Why Recycling Is Garbage," *Forbes*, November 17, 1997. |
| John Tierney | "Recycling Is Garbage," *New York Times Magazine*, June 30, 1996. |
| Alexander Volokh and Lynn Scarlett | "Is Recycling Good or Bad—or Both?" *Consumers' Research Magazine*, September 1997. |
| Jesse Walker and Pierre Desrochers | "Recycling Is an Economic Activity, Not a Moral Imperative," *American Enterprise*, January/February 1999. |

# CHAPTER 3

# Is Toxic Waste Disposal a Serious Problem?

# Chapter Preface

In 1986, a barge named the *Khian Sea* left the territorial waters of the United States and began looking for a place to dump its cargo: fourteen thousand tons of toxic incinerator ash from Philadelphia. The barge traveled to the Bahamas, the Dominican Republic, Honduras, Bermuda, Guinea-Bissau, and the Netherlands Antilles, but at each port its cargo was rejected. The environmental organization Greenpeace had been telling potential recipients of the ash that the toxic cargo posed a threat to human health. Finally, unwitting officials in Haiti accepted the ash, which the ship's crew had called "fertilizer," and the waste was dumped onto a beach in the town of Gonaives. That same day, city officials learned of the scam and ordered the waste returned to the ship. But in the middle of the night, the *Khian Sea* slipped away, leaving the ash on the beach. There it remained for more than a decade before environmental and social groups forced the U.S. government and entrepreneurs to remove and properly dispose of it.

The *Khian Sea* incident publicized the toxic waste trade and made possible the 1989 Basel Convention on the Control of Transboundary Movements of Hazardous Wastes and Their Disposal—an international body that regulates toxic waste trading between nations. One significant outcome of the Basel Convention has been a ban—referred to as the North to South ban—on toxic waste shipments from rich nations such as the United States to poor nations such as Haiti.

Underlying the Basel Convention is the belief that polluters should be held responsible for their own pollution. Those involved in the Convention argue that for too long, rich nations have reaped the benefits of industrialization but have not paid all the environmental costs associated with it. The Convention's tenets are based on democratic principles, which not only emphasize the rights of individuals but their responsibilities as well. Also central to democracy is the equal treatment of individuals. Environmentalists concerned about toxic waste dumping call this kind of democratic equality "environmental justice." Environmentalists believe that poor people of color should not bear an unfair proportion of the world's pollution.

Although most environmentalists hail the Basel Convention as an important step toward environmental justice, they point out that the North to South ban only regulates waste trading between nations. According to these commentators, "environmental racism" still goes on within nations. For example, Debby Katz, director of the Citizens Awareness Network, an organization that works to stop environmental pollution in the United States, asserts, "Communities chosen to suffer contamination are routinely poor, rural, and people of color." Katz and other activists call such communities "sacrifice zones," places that have little money and political power to fight corporate polluters. As Greenpeace activist Marcelo Furtado contends, "The waste trade follows the path of least resistance. The poorer and less informed the community (or country), the more likely it is to become a target for [toxic waste] traders." Just as the Basel Convention has prohibited rich, developed nations from dumping on poor, undeveloped nations, efforts by many U.S. activists are focused on stopping toxic waste dumping on America's poorest communities.

The *Khian Sea* dumping inspired a new generation of activists seeking environmental justice. As the barge's saga illustrates, toxic waste poses a potential threat to the health of people everywhere and, as some activists contend, endangers some people more than others.

*"The total number of [toxic waste cleanup] sites that have had their cleanup goals met through remediation activities increases each year."*

# Hazardous Waste Cleanup Projects Have Been Successful

U.S. Environmental Protection Agency

The U.S. Environmental Protection Agency (EPA) is the federal agency that oversees enforcement of federal laws governing pollution and environmental hazards. The EPA asserts in the following viewpoint that the Superfund program—the common name for the 1980 Comprehensive Environmental, Response, Compensation, and Liability Act (CERCLA)—has succeeded in cleaning up most toxic waste sites on its priority list. According to the agency's environmental indicators, human populations living near toxic waste sites have been protected, numerous sites have been completely remediated, and toxic waste has been successfully treated and disposed of. Furthermore, the EPA claims that the Superfund program is growing more successful each year.

As you read, consider the following questions:

1. What is the Superfund's mission, as stated by the EPA?
2. According to the agency, why does the EPA collect and report environmental indicators?
3. What additional environmental indicators is the EPA developing in order to measure the progress of the Superfund program?

Excerpted from "Cleanup of Hazardous Waste Sites," by the U.S. Environmental Protection Agency, www.epa.gov, October 3, 2000.

In the late 1970s, a series of news stories alerted the United States to the dangers of dumping, burying, or improperly storing hazardous waste. Waste dumped for more than 25 years at the Love Canal site in Niagara Falls, New York, began to contaminate streams and soil, threatening the health of the local community. The Valley of the Drums site in Brook, Kentucky, was found to contain thousands of leaking storage barrels. In both of these cases, public health and the surrounding environment were threatened, and lives were disrupted.

## Superfund

Congress passed the Comprehensive Environmental, Response, Compensation, and Liability Act (CERCLA) in 1980 in response to the threat from uncontrolled disposal of hazardous wastes in the country. CERCLA, commonly known as Superfund, was the first comprehensive federal law designed specifically to deal with the dangers of the nation's abandoned and uncontrolled hazardous waste sites. Under the Superfund program, the U.S. Environmental Protection Agency's (EPA) mission is to:

- protect human health and the environment from uncontrolled hazardous releases;
- study, design, and construct long-term solutions for the nation's most serious hazardous waste problems; and
- make polluters pay for cleaning up the contamination they created.

The Superfund program is an ambitious and complex environmental program because it must address each site's unique characteristics, including multiple contaminants (e.g., creosotes and heavy metals such as lead and mercury) and various contaminated media (e.g., water, air, and soil). EPA collects and compiles a wide variety of information about the progress of cleanup at each Superfund site. Some of this information is used as "Environmental Indicators" of the progress being made to reduce to safe levels or eliminate entirely the risks posed by contaminants at these sites.

## What Are Hazardous Waste Sites?

It is difficult to describe a "typical" hazardous waste site. Each site is unique and may have had many past uses. Many

## Past Superfund Site Uses

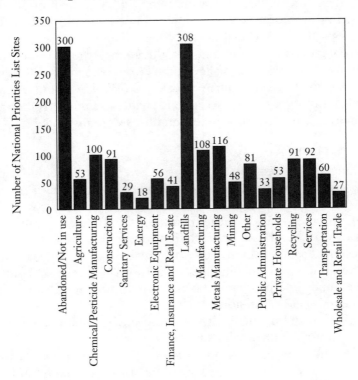

U.S. Environmental Protection Agency, 2000.

Superfund sites were municipal or industrial landfills, or manufacturing plants where operators improperly disposed of waste, but Superfund sites span a wide range of past uses.

Although many of Superfund's hazardous waste sites have been abandoned, they may exist in active industrial or commercial areas. Some are large federal facilities with "hot spots" of contamination from various high-tech or military activities.

## When Are Sites Added to the National Priorities List (NPL)?

Because there are numerous hazardous waste sites across the nation, EPA must identify and prioritize those sites based on the relative risks they pose. To assess these risks, EPA uses a mathematical scoring system called the Hazard

Ranking System (HRS). HRS scores are based on the likelihood that a hazardous substance will be released, the toxicity and amount of hazardous substances, and the location of populations potentially affected by the contamination. A site's HRS score will determine if it is eligible for placement on the National Priorities List (NPL), the list of the sites with the greatest risks, which are eligible for cleanup using federal money.

The NPL tracks the Superfund program's progress in cleaning up hazardous waste sites. Each year, through a series of updates to the Federal Register, the NPL changes with new sites proposed, added, and deleted from the list. As of March 2000, 1,485 sites were on the NPL.

## What Are Non-NPL Sites?

Keep in mind that NPL sites are only a small subset of a much larger Superfund inventory of hazardous waste sites. In addition to the 1,485 NPL sites, this hazardous waste site inventory also includes 41,442 non-NPL sites and sites that have no further remedial action planned (NFRAP). Non-NPL sites pose health and environmental risks that can be addressed through short-term cleanups. They do not require the complex cleanup needed at NPL sites. NFRAP sites are those at which no further Superfund remedial assessment work is required, based on currently available information. Of these 41,442 sites, approximately 23% are non-NPL sites, while 77% have been archived as NFRAP sites.

## What Types of Contaminants Are Found at Hazardous Waste Sites?

The types of contamination resulting from past site activities can vary widely. Some of the contaminants most frequently found at Superfund sites include:
- heavy metals such as lead and mercury;
- volatile organic compounds (VOCs);
- polychlorinated biphenyls (PCBs);
- pesticides and herbicides; and
- creosotes.

Such contaminants can have adverse effects on human

health, causing breathing difficulties, developmental and learning disorders, and chronic health conditions such as cancer. They also pose a threat to ecosystems because they can affect the ability of animals and plants to survive and reproduce. . . .

## How Many People Live Near NPL Sites and What Are the Risks?

Currently, there are more than 6 million people living within one mile of the 1,474 NPL sites, and 76 million living within four miles of these sites. However, just living near a site does not automatically place a person at risk. Risk depends on the amount and toxicity of contaminants present and if a person comes in contact with them (e.g., by drinking contaminated water, breathing contaminated air, or trespassing on the site).

To determine the amounts and types of chemicals being released at sites, EPA performs human health and ecological risk assessments. Human health risk assessments examine the type and amount of contamination; how people might be exposed, how much exposure could occur and what the short and long-term effects of that exposure might be. Ecological risk assessments are similar to human health risk assessments. However, they are performed for ecological resources including animals and plants. EPA also tests for the pathways of exposure (i.e., ways people can be exposed—inhalation, ingestion, or absorption through skin) to these chemicals and the threats these chemicals pose to human health and the environment. Data are collected through site investigations, field sampling, and historical research. These risk assessments help facilitate risk-management decisions. They also determine long-term cleanup goals. This ensures that the selected cleanup remedy protects the public and surrounding ecosystems.

## What Are Environmental Indicators?

Environmental Indicators are specific measures of program performance used to assess progress toward cleaning up a hazardous waste site. EPA collects and reports Environmental Indicators data to:

- show and identify trends in human activities that impact the environment;
- show and identify trends in changes in the environment;
- establish relationships among environmental variables, such as the nature and extent of hazardous wastes and various media;
- measure and communicate environmental achievement and progress (or lack of progress) made towards a goal; and
- help to guide its strategic planning and budget decisions.

## What Are Superfund's Environmental Indicators?

Superfund Environmental Indicators are used to measure the progress made in protecting human health and the environment through site cleanup activities. To date, three Environmental Indicators have been developed and implemented. These indicators are described below:

- *Populations Protected (Indicator A)*

  Indicator A measures the environmental progress made in protecting people living near NPL and non-NPL hazardous waste sites from: (1) immediate threats that removals address, and (2) long-term threats that remedial actions (long-term cleanups) address.

  To alleviate existing or immediate threats to people at risk, EPA often takes short-term cleanup actions to control these critical situations and ensure people's safety. Following the short-term cleanup actions, EPA takes additional actions to minimize or permanently remove hazardous contamination. Because these actions often take more time to complete than short-term cleanup actions, they are called long-term cleanup actions.

  To protect people during short-term and long-term cleanup activities, EPA may take one or a combination of the following actions to address immediate threats posed by a site:

  - provide alternate sources of drinking water to people;
  - relocate people (i.e., move them to a location where they are not at risk);
  - use site security measures, such as erecting a fence to restrict access to a site;

- provide institutional controls like deed restrictions; or
- conduct removal or remedial actions that remove, stabilize, or consolidate wastes or otherwise protect residents or workers by reducing pathways of exposure.

For each type of action taken by EPA, Indicator A counts or measures: (1) the number of hazardous waste sites where the action was taken, and (2) the number of people protected as a result of the action. For example:

- *If alternative drinking water was provided:* Indicator A reports the number of sites and the number of people at each site where:
  - alternate drinking water was permanently provided;
  - alternate drinking water was temporarily provided; or
  - the water supply was reinstated.
- *If people were relocated:* Indicator A reports the number of sites and the number of people at each site where people were:
  - permanently relocated;
  - temporarily relocated; or
  - returned to their original location.
- *If site access was restricted:*
  - access was restricted using fencing;
  - access was restricted using guards; or
  - access was restricted in some other fashion.
- *Achieving Permanent Cleanup Goals (Indicator B)*
  Hazardous substances can contaminate several environmental media (e.g., land, surface water, groundwater, air) at the same time.

  Indicator B measures the progress made toward meeting permanent cleanup goals for each contaminated medium at each NPL site or non-NPL site. As these media cleanup goals are met, it is possible to document the progress being made toward overall site cleanup, and ultimately deletion of the site from the NPL.

  The levels of goal attainment used to describe the progress made toward meeting permanent cleanup goals for each contaminated medium are:
  - *Cleanup underway:* Goals have not yet been attained, but on-site work has been started and is ongoing;

- *Partially achieved:* All goals have been achieved for a specific operable unit (each distinct cleanup activity addressing a separate form of contamination under-taken as part of a Superfund site cleanup is called an operable unit). However, all goals for all operable units have not been achieved for a particular affected medium; and
- *Fully achieved:* All goals for a medium have been attained.

Soil cleanup is often achieved first because it typically involves excavation and removal of contaminated soil for treatment or disposal at an off-site location. Groundwater remediation usually takes longer because of the complexity of removing contaminants from underground aquifers that hold groundwater. Meanwhile, surface water cleanup typically involves removing and treating contamination that settles to the bottom of streams or other bodies of water.

- *Cleanup Technologies Applied (Indicator C)*
This indicator measures the amount of contaminated materials that have been treated, stabilized, protected against, or removed at NPL and non-NPL sites through the use of risk-management technologies, engineering techniques, and institutional controls.

Two cleanup technologies most often used are treatment and containment.
  - *Treatment technologies* are used to reduce the toxicity, mobility, and/or volume of wastes found at sites. An example is bioremediation, which is a treatment technology that uses bacteria to degrade toxic waste into harmless by-products. Bioremediation is useful for treating chemical spills.
  - *Containment technologies* create a physical barrier that holds the contamination in place. The barrier protects the public from any threat of direct contact. Capping is an example of a containment technology, which involves the construction of a protective barrier over contaminated soil, solid waste, or sediment.

At most NPL sites, complex long-term remedial actions are needed to clean up contaminants in order to restore the affected area to designated cleanup levels. A key aspect of site cleanup is the determination of the types and amounts of hazardous waste that must be removed. Indicator C:

- measures the amount of contaminated materials that has been treated, stabilized, or removed at NPL and non-NPL sites using cleanup technologies.
- measures the volume of waste handled, which aids in understanding the amount of effort necessary to achieve cleanup goals and deletion of a site from the NPL.

EPA Headquarters has been collecting Environmental Indicators information from the EPA Regions since 1989. . . .

## What Do Environmental Indicators Explain?

To provide a clear picture of the progress being made at Superfund sites, we use the data from (1) completed short-term cleanups known as site removals (both at NPL and non-NPL sites) and (2) from long-term cleanups called site re-

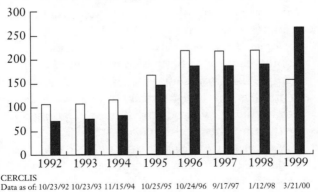

**Indicator B: NPL Sites Where Cleanup Goals Have Been Met Through Long-Term Actions from 1992 to March 2000**

CERCLIS
Data as of: 10/23/92 10/23/93 11/15/94  10/25/95  10/24/96  9/17/97  1/12/98  3/21/00

☐ Cleanup Underway        ■ Sites Fully Cleaned

At any given site, more than one area may be contaminated.
Numbers represent cumulative totals since inception.

mediations. Based on this information, Indicators A, B, and C tell us the following:

*Addressing Immediate Threats—Indicator A*

Through March 2000, the Superfund program had supplied more than 430,000 people with alternate sources of drinking water to prevent them from consuming contaminated drinking water. More than 30,000 people have been relocated when contamination posed the most severe immediate threats. To prohibit certain types of uses at sites, institutional controls, such as deed restrictions and access restrictions, have been implemented at more than 600 NPL sites. Site security measures, such as fencing and guards, to restrict access have been implemented at more than 500 NPL sites. In addition, removals/remedial actions have occurred at 1,222 NPL sites.

*Achieving Permanent Cleanup Goals—Indicator B*

The total number of Superfund sites that have had their cleanup goals met through remediation activities increases each year. In the last eight years for example, the total number of NPL sites that have met all cleanup goals for at least one area of medium has more than tripled.

*Cleanup Technologies Applied—Indicator C*

Since the Superfund program began in 1980, tremendous volumes of hazardous waste have been handled, treated or disposed. . . .

Cleanup experts also have applied 2,900 treatment actions and 4,200 containment actions at NPL sites since 1980. In addition, 6,200 other actions, such as access restrictions, institutional controls, discharges, and disposals, which cannot be readily categorized as treatment or containment technologies, have also been used at these sites to protect populations.

## What Can Additional Indicators Reveal?

The Superfund program will continue to make important strides in meeting the environmental cleanup challenges of the future. While Indicators A, B, and C address many aspects of hazardous waste sites, additional indicators are being developed to measure the progress made in reducing human health risk (Indicator D), protecting ecological resources (Indicator E), and returning land to productive use (Indicator L).

> *"It has not proven possible to clean up [contaminated] areas, certainly not to pristine conditions, and in most cases, not even to the point of compliance with established health standards."*

# Hazardous Waste Cleanup Projects Usually Fail

R. Allan Freeze

R. Allan Freeze maintains in the following viewpoint that scientists currently lack the expertise to contain or remove the source of contamination at hazardous waste sites. According to Freeze, trying to contain the source of contamination by installing costly pump-and-treat systems usually fails to remove sufficient quantities of contaminants. Furthermore, he claims that removing the contaminated soil and transporting it elsewhere simply relocates the problem. R. Allan Freeze, former professor and director in the Geological Engineering Program at the University of British Columbia, is the coauthor of *Groundwater Contamination: Optimal Capture and Containment*.

As you read, consider the following questions:
1. According to Freeze, how do pump-and-treat systems operate?
2. Why is it so difficult to remove NAPLs from contaminated groundwater, as stated by Freeze?
3. As related by the author, why is treating contaminated groundwater problematic?

Excerpted from *The Environmental Pendulum: A Quest for the Truth About Toxic Chemicals, Human Health, and Environmental Protection*, by R. Allan Freeze (Berkeley: University of California Press, 2000). Copyright © 2000 by R. Allan Freeze. Reprinted with permission.

There is no question what the members of the public want at contaminated sites. They want them "cleaned up." They want them returned to the pristine conditions that existed before they were fouled by evil polluters. They want every last drop of contaminant sucked back out of the ground. They want their groundwater cleansed of all contamination and protected from the threat of all future contamination.

## Site Restoration Through Contaminant Removal

Legislators at both the state and federal level have heard the message loud and clear. Almost all the early legislation, including the Superfund legislation [the 1980 Comprehensive Environmental, Response, Compensation, and Liability Act (CERCLA)], assumed that the goal of remedial activities was complete cleanup, or at least cleanup to a level that met all applicable health standards. It was assumed that these standards would be met at every contaminated site targeted for cleanup, and at each site they would be met both in the source area and throughout the plume [the area polluted by the dissolved contaminant]. The problem was viewed as having two parts: remove the source areas, and shrink the plumes. Early programmatic goals did not question whether this could be done: they simply specified how many sites would be cleaned up under the anticipated budgets, and on what schedule.

It is hard to find fault with this way of thinking. It is in the tradition of American "can do" optimism. There is only one problem: the optimism was misplaced. It has not proven possible to clean up source areas, certainly not to pristine conditions, and in most cases, not even to the point of compliance with established health standards. The early goals were laudable, but they have turned out to be neither economically nor technically feasible.

The agents of fate in this case are the dreaded DNAPLs [dense, non-aqueous-phase liquids]. These are the free-product liquid contaminants—solvents, wood-preserving chemicals, PCB-laced oils, and pesticides—which are denser than water, and which residualize themselves below the water table in pools, blobs, and droplets within the pores and fractures of the subsurface soils and rocks. The great majority of contaminated sites in North America, and especially those of industrial origin, have residualized DNAPLs in their source area. It is our inability to remove all of the DNAPL from the subsurface, or for that matter to even locate where it all is, that has rendered most contaminated sites impossible to clean up. There are simply no current technologies that will remove every last droplet from the subsurface soils and rocks. Unfortunately, as we shall see shortly, if the source areas threaten drinking-water aquifers, then it *is necessary* to remove almost every last droplet to prevent the formation of contaminant plumes that will snake their way through these aquifers at concentrations that exceed the health standards.

My colleague John Cherry has referred to DNAPL sites as having "terminal cancer." Carrying the analogy further, he identifies the source area as the locus of the disease, the "tumor," if you will, and the plume that emanates from the source area as the "symptom." As we shall see, scientists have learned how to treat the symptoms, but as yet they have no cure for the disease.

## Types of Remedial Measures

In order to get a feeling for the types of remedial measures that come under consideration at contaminated sites, we will turn to a case history. Price's Landfill, near Atlantic City, New Jersey, bears many similarities to the Ville Mercier case history. Like the one at Ville Mercier [in Quebec, Canada], the landfill was developed in an old sand-and-gravel quarry, and it operated in the period 1969 to 1976, before the inappropriateness of such sites was widely recognized. It accepted both solid municipal waste and liquid chemical waste, and as at Ville Mercier, there is anecdotal evidence of tanker trucks opening their spigots directly into the quarry. Price's Landfill sits over the Cohansey aquifer, about one mile west of a well field that is the primary source of water supply for the Atlantic City Municipal Water Authority. It was recognized in the late seventies that the aquifer was being contaminated by the landfill. At least one of the city pumping wells was closed down as early as 1981 under threat of contamination.

In general, approaches [to clean up the site] fall into one

of three categories: accept the risk, contain the contamination, or try to remove it.

If we decide to accept the risk, what is usually meant is that the risk is so small that we choose to do nothing about it. There are some waste-management facilities that have been fortuitously constructed in favorable hydrogeological settings, which may indeed offer very little risk to potable water supplies. In such circumstances, it may be societally optimal to accept the do-nothing option.

---

## Superfund Is Costly and Unfair

The [Superfund] program has not worked as intended. Small businesses and charitable organizations such as the Girl Scouts have been hauled into court [because they are responsible for cleaning up their property even though they bought it already contaminated]; large corporations who have contributed only a small amount of hazardous waste have been liable for the lion's share of the cleanup because of their deep pockets; banks have been held liable only because they have mortgages on the land; and municipalities have been forced into hiring lawyers where their limited resources could be better used to upgrade essential citizen services.

Blanche Lambert Lincoln, quoted in Mary H. Cooper, *CQ Researcher*, August 23, 1996.

---

The risk at Price's Landfill was not small enough to consider a do-nothing option. However, we might still accept the risk in a sense if we were to decide to accept the contaminated conditions in the aquifer without attempting any remedial program in the aquifer or at the landfill. Now, it is not likely that anyone would accept the contaminated groundwater as an untreated source of supply, so there are two further options that fall under this category. We could treat the water at the wellhead (which was not considered at Price's Landfill), or we could try to develop an alternative source of supply (which for Price's Landfill was costed out at $8.5 to $11.3 million in 1980 dollars).

## Contain the Source

For those sites where contaminant plumes have entered drinking-water aquifers, and where wellhead treatment or the development of alternate sources of supply are not acceptable options, one is left with two possibilities: try to contain the source and control the plume, or try to remove the source. Containment options are divided into those involving surface control, those employing physical barriers and cutoff walls, and those based on plume management. Surface control measures such as grading and capping are carried out at most contaminated sites as part of the remedial package, but not usually as the primary thrust. At many sites, physical barriers have been constructed around source areas. The technology now exists to install such barriers to depths of tens of feet (or even hundreds of feet in favorable geologic materials).

By far the most common remedial action has involved the installation of pump-and-treat systems wherein contaminated water is pumped from afflicted aquifers, treated to remove the contaminants, and then either used as a water supply, reinjected back into the aquifer, or released into lakes or streams. As we shall soon see, pumping water from plume areas can be effective in controlling plume migration, whereas pumping from source areas is seldom effective in removing contaminant mass.

## Remove the Source

The only contaminant removal technology that has ever really proven itself is excavation. What could be simpler, after all, than digging up the source areas and removing the "tumors." NIMBY [Not In My Backyard] groups usually demand it, and regulatory agencies looking for simple solutions that will solve problems once and for all, often embrace it. For very small volumes of contaminated material, like those associated with leaking underground storage tanks, the excavation option makes good sense, but for larger contaminated sites of the Superfund variety, excavation is simply too expensive. For Price's Landfill, which at twenty-two acres is actually a very small landfill, that excavation is by far the most expensive option at $12.7 million. (And remember, these are 1980 dollars; current costs would be double or more.) At Ville Mercier, which is a bigger site, cost estimates for the excavation option ran greater than $100 million. When one begins to see cost estimates of this size, while remembering the tens of thousands of sites that exist around the country, it is reasonable to question whether the societal risk reductions achieved can possibly be worth the expense.

There is another issue associated with excavation: what to do with the excavated material. Most remedial plans specify that the excavated material should be taken to a "secure landfill." However, even the most secure landfill is secure only in the short term. One can easily conjure up visions of waste excavated from one site and placed in another, only to require reexcavation and reemplacement once again a few tens of years down the road. It sounds like a wonderful plan for the waste-excavation companies, but I doubt that it is optimal for society at large.

Lastly, there is the question of whether excavation necessarily reduces health risk. At Ville Mercier, for example, risk analyses indicated that the additional health risks that would be borne by local residents and on-site workers during the excavation process would be greater than those associated with just leaving the contamination in place. The activities associated with digging up toxic waste, transporting it across the countryside, and reemplacing it somewhere else are not risk-free. . . .

## The Sad Tale of Pump-and-Treat

In the naive glow of the "can do" period following the passage of the Superfund legislation in the early 1980s, hundreds of pump-and-treat systems were put in place at contaminated sites across the nation. The idea was simple: put some wells in the ground; pump out all the contaminated liquids; treat them to remove the contaminants; and walk away. The engineering work plans for these early projects are full of optimistic calculations of the amount of time required to attain the desired cleanup standards. Most consultants and contractors promised their clients that they would be off the hook within a few months, or at most a few years.

It was not to be. The reality has been a sad tale of failure and frustration. Pump-and-treat has been so ineffective in removing contaminants from the subsurface that the results are almost laughable. At Ville Mercier for example, three wells have been pumping since 1984 at a combined rate of

700 gallons per minute. In the first eight and a half years of operation these wells pumped almost 3 billion gallons of water out of the ground. This contaminated water was then sent through a treatment plant at a cost of about $1 million per year. And what was accomplished? The total amount of all chemicals removed from the subsurface has been about 13,000 gallons, less than 0.001 percent of the water pumped. More important, the estimated volume of chemicals in the ground at Ville Mercier runs to about 4.5 million gallons, which means that the amount of chemical removed in eight and a half years of pumping is less than 1 percent of that still remaining in the ground. The cost of removal has been $650 per gallon, which is probably about one thousand times more than the chemicals were worth in the first place.

Results from across North America tell the same story. Pumping wells on the Kodak property in Rochester, New York, pump more than 5 million gallons of water per year in order to retrieve less than 1,000 gallons of TCE and methylene chloride. At the Fairchild semiconductor site in California, pumping more than a billion gallons of water per year recovers less than 2,000 gallons per year of acetone and xylene.

## Toxic Villains

As you have probably suspected by now, the villains in this piece are the LNAPLs [light non-aqueous-phase liquids] and DNAPLs floating around in the groundwater beneath the sites. Pumping wells designed to pump water are simply not effective in capturing NAPLs. Some of the pumping wells in the early pump-and-treat systems were actually designed to recover NAPL pools directly. In the early years there were many articles in the technical literature suggesting various strategies to optimize direct NAPL recovery. Time and experience have taught us that even this seemingly straightforward objective is not viable. The NAPLs tend to be distributed irregularly throughout the source area in small pockets and globules not easily isolated or recovered. When the pumps are turned on, the groundwater comes into the well preferentially relative to the free-product chemicals. The residualized NAPLs resist dislodging from the nooks and crannies where they have settled; the sorbed

NAPLs remain glommed onto the organic matter that now acts as their host. The water pumped out, whether it be from a plume area or a source area, contains dissolved contaminants, but because the solubilities of most of these chemicals are very low, the mass of chemical removed is just a minuscule percentage of the water pumped. Even when the contaminant concentrations are very low (measuring just a few parts per billion), they may exceed the very conservative health standards that have been set, and all the pumped water must therefore be sent through the very expensive treatment facilities.

In 1990, the Environmental Protection Agency (EPA) carried out a review of a large number of the pump-and-treat facilities operating under the Superfund legislation. The agency's findings were uniform across the nation. Contaminant concentrations in affected aquifers are sometimes reduced by pump-and-treat activities, but the rate of reduction tapers off as pumping proceeds; and if the pumps are stopped, concentrations usually return to their original levels. All cases show massive volumes of water pumped for minuscule contaminant recoveries. The time estimates for "cleanup" were universally optimistic. In fact, it is now recognized that at most of these sites cleanup goals will never be achieved through pump-and-treat alone.

## Exotic Cocktails

It is not only the pumping end of the pump-and-treat game that is problematical. So too is the treatment end. The removal of organic chemicals from water is not a simple or straightforward task. If the contamination is limited to a single chemical, chances for success are better. Some chemicals, being volatile, are easily removed through air stripping. Others that are strongly sorbed to organic matter can be removed from the water through carbon absorption technologies. In most cases, however, contamination does not consist of a single chemical. Most source areas contain a cocktail of chemicals, all with different physical and chemical properties. It is difficult and expensive to design treatment plants that can strip out all these contaminants together. At Ville Mercier, for example, where the cocktail was particularly exotic, the $1-million-per-year treatment plant was actually quite inefficient, and the "treated" water that came out the end of the system was really only partially treated. Concentrations of many of the chemicals still exceeded health standards. Nevertheless, with regulatory approval, this water was released into a nearby surface stream. It is likely (although by no means sure) that the natural groundwater flow would have delivered the contaminated groundwater to this same stream eventually, but there is no question that it got there faster through the hand of man than it would have through the hand of nature.

*"The best solution for the future is that no more nuclear waste should be produced anywhere in the world."*

# Nuclear Waste Disposal Is a Serious Problem

Greenpeace

Greenpeace is an environmental organization that opposes nuclear energy and the use of toxic chemicals. In the following viewpoint, Greenpeace contends that no safe methods have been developed to dispose of the radioactive waste produced by nuclear power plants. According to the organization, the most popular solution is to bury nuclear waste, but buried waste can release harmful gas into the air and leach into underground waters. Greenpeace argues that as more nuclear power plants are shut down, the amount of radioactive waste that must be disposed of will increase, heightening the risk of contamination.

As you read, consider the following questions:

1. According to Greenpeace, what are the differences between high level, intermediate level, and low level nuclear waste?
2. Why might "spent" fuel force the closure of numerous nuclear power plants, as stated by Greenpeace?
3. According to the organization, what methods have some countries devised to dismantle nuclear reactors?

As part of the routine operation of every nuclear power station some waste materials are discharged directly into the environment. Liquid waste is discharged with 'turbine cooling water' into the sea or a nearby river, and gaseous waste is released into the atmosphere.

## Three Types of Nuclear Waste

There are three categories of radioactive nuclear waste: High level waste (HLW), Intermediate level Waste (ILW) and Low level waste (LLW).

HLW consists mainly of irradiated fuel from the cores of nuclear reactors (although the nuclear industry does not consider this to be a waste), and the high level liquid waste produced during reprocessing. The removal of plutonium by reprocessing results in a huge volume of this liquid radioactive waste. Some of this deadly reprocessing waste, stored in large tanks, is mixed with a hot glass material and solidified, with the resulting glass logs also being classified as HLW. While the glassification process may make it easier to transport and store the nuclear waste, it does not in any way diminish the terrible danger posed to the public and the environment for millennia to come. HLW is typically a thousand times more radioactive than ILW.

ILW consists mainly of metal fuel 'cans' which originally contained the uranium fuel for nuclear power stations, reactor metalwork and chemical residues. It has to be shielded to protect workers and the public from exposure during transport and disposal. It is usually stored at the site of production. ILW is typically a thousand times more radioactive that LLW.

LLW can be defined as waste which does not require shielding during normal handling and transportation. LLW consists mainly of items such as protective clothing and laboratory equipment which may have come into contact with radioactive material.

## Disposal of Radioactive Wastes

The highly radioactive nuclear fuel is removed from the reactor and at most sites this "spent" fuel is being stored temporarily in water-filled cooling pools. As the cooling pools of many reactors are rapidly being filled, many reactors may soon have to shut down due to a lack of storage space for the deadly waste. According to estimates by the International Atomic Energy Agency (IAEA), the global amount of spent fuel was 125,000 tonnes in 1992, and this will rise to 200,000 tonnes by the year 2000, and to 450,000 by the middle of the 21st century. Yet, although a variety of disposal methods have been under discussion for decades—including disposal in space—there is still no solution for what to do with nuclear waste.

Oliver. © 1998 by Gary Oliver. Reprinted with permission.

Most of the current proposed 'solutions' for dealing with nuclear waste involve burying it underground in a special store with strong enough protection to stop its radioactivity escaping. The nuclear industry purports that after some form of processing, burial in the ground or the seabed will be sufficiently safe. This philosophy was born largely under the pressures of having to convince a worried public that the nuclear industry knows how to dispose of its wastes. However, this is a false assurance.

To pretend, as the nuclear industry often does, that a few

experiments, test bores or geological surveys is all that is needed to deal with radioactive waste is simply disingenuous or scientifically illiterate or possibly both. Adequate proof will take tens of thousands of years.

## The Two Main Dangers: Air and Water Contamination

### Air Contamination

Explosive or slow releases of gases from an underground disposal site is theoretically possible. There is unfortunately no reliable way of estimating this danger—there are too many uncertainties concerning actual methods of burial and of possible chemical interactions within a real environment.

### Water Contamination

This is generally taken as the most likely mechanism of pollution in connection with waste disposal in rock. Underground waters may come in contact with radioactive elements that have leached out from the waste and contaminate the drinking water of local and distant communities.

In addition to underground burial, various on-site storage schemes are being investigated. Of primary interest is the storage of the spent fuel in large steel or concrete containers. While on-site storage of spent fuel keeps the material at the point of its creation and reduces transportation risks, hundreds of communities around the world are threatened with de facto high level dumps on their doorsteps. Plans also exist for consolidating containerised spent fuel at a few above-ground regional facilities, resulting in a huge number of road transports in containers not designed to withstand credible accidents.

*The best solution for the future is that no more nuclear waste should be produced anywhere in the world.*

## Dismantling Nuclear Power Stations

Large quantities of nuclear waste are also produced when a nuclear reactor is shutdown. This is because many of its component parts, including the fuel, have become radioactive. They cannot simply be thrown away. The process of dealing with the power station at this point is called "decommissioning." Apart from removing the used fuel, however, there is not a clear agreement about what should happen next. No full-size reactor has yet been fully dismantled anywhere in the world. Although some countries are planning to remove the entire structure, including the radioactive parts, leaving a flat empty space, others have suggested leaving the building where it stands, covering it in concrete or possibly burying it under a mound of earth.

The cost of decommissioning nuclear power reactors is highly speculative. Cost estimates have been derived from generic studies, from scaling up the costs of decommissioning smaller research facilities. The detail and sophistication employed in developing these estimates varies greatly and their lack of standardisation makes comparisons difficult. Moreover, limited decommissioning experience—none with large reactors—makes it impossible to know if the estimates are on target, but it has been suggested that decommissioning costs could be up to 100% of the initial cost of construction.

During the next three decades, more than 350 nuclear reactors will be taken out of service. Yet more than 40 years after the first nuclear power plant started producing electricity the nuclear industry still has no answers on how to safely and cost effectively dismantle a reactor.

*"By reducing, eliminating, or managing their waste, nuclear facilities have prevented or lessened adverse impacts on water, land, habitat, species, and air."*

# Nuclear Waste Disposal Is Not a Serious Problem

Nuclear Energy Institute

The Nuclear Energy Institute (NEI) is the policy organization of the nuclear energy and technologies industry. In the following viewpoint, NEI claims that nuclear waste does not pose a threat to the environment because it is handled with extreme care. According to the organization, the relatively small amount of waste created as a byproduct of nuclear energy generation is safely stored on-site or carefully transported to off-site locations. NEI maintains that used nuclear fuel is nonexplosive and nonflammable and can be safely stored in specially designed transportation containers.

As you read, consider the following questions:

1. Why does NEI believe that the federal government will be able to dispose of nuclear waste safely in the future?
2. According to the organization, how does the federal government ensure that nuclear fuel containers adequately contain nuclear waste?
3. How is nuclear waste transported, as related by NEI?

Excerpted from "Protecting the Environment," by the Nuclear Energy Institute, www.nei.org, 2001. Copyright © 2001 by the Nuclear Energy Institute. Reprinted with permission.

Of all energy sources, nuclear energy has perhaps the lowest impact on the environment especially in relation to kilowatts produced because nuclear plants do not emit harmful gases, require a relatively small area, and effectively mitigate other impacts. In other words, nuclear energy is the most "eco-efficient" of all energy sources because it produces the most electricity in relation to its minimal environmental impact. There are no significant adverse effects to water, land, habitat, species and air resources. . . .

## Safe, Effective Hazardous Waste Management

*Total waste management.* The environmental policies and practices at nuclear power plants are unique in having successfully prevented significant harmful impacts to the environment since the start of the commercial nuclear industry more than 40 years ago. As a result, the nuclear energy industry is the only industry established since the industrial revolution that has managed and accounted for virtually all of its by-product material. By reducing, eliminating, or managing their waste, nuclear facilities have prevented or lessened adverse impacts on water, land, habitat, species, and air from releases or emissions in the production of electricity. Throughout the nuclear fuel cycle, the small volumes of waste byproducts actually created are carefully contained, packaged and safely stored. As a result of improved process efficiencies, the average volume of waste generated at nuclear power plants has decreased significantly in the past two decades.

*Relatively small volume of high-level waste.* The high-level waste actually produced, in the form of used fuel rods, on average totals less than 20 tons per nuclear plant annually. Uranium is a very dense material, heavy but low in volume. The trillions of kilowatt-hours of nuclear electricity generated over more than 40 years have produced about 40,000 tons of used fuel rods. These rods, if stacked together, would fill a football field to a depth of a little more than four yards. To put this in perspective, all of U.S. industry produces 300,000 tons of hazardous waste annually.

*Used fuel safely stored on-site.* From the start of the commercial nuclear era with the Atomic Energy Act in 1954, it has been national policy that the federal government should retain control of, and be responsible for, the ultimate disposal of used nuclear material. This policy was reaffirmed in the Nuclear Waste Policy Act of 1982 and its 1987 amendments. Implementation of these policies has been delayed, and used fuel remains stored at plant sites under strict containment requirements, with no adverse environmental impacts. Despite the delays in the federal program, scientific investigation of a permanent disposal site is well advanced. The scientific and technical issues are well understood, and there is no reason the United States cannot develop the necessary infrastructure for transportation, storage and disposal of used nuclear fuel.

*Life-cycle analysis reveals nuclear energy's environmental benefits.* To place waste byproducts and emissions from all forms of power generation into perspective requires "life-cycle" analysis. This form of analysis provides a complete picture of a source's total impact on the environment—on land, air, water, wildlife. Because of nuclear energy's success in preventing adverse environmental impacts, especially in the management of used fuel, life-cycle analyses demonstrate that nuclear energy is one of the "greenest" forms of electricity available. A sound, scientific process such as life-cycle analysis, if employed uniformly, would prevent misleading environmental claims and promote consumer confidence in electricity choices as the market moves toward competition.

## The Safe Transportation of Used Nuclear Fuel

*Small amount of waste carefully managed.* The high-level waste currently produced by all U.S. nuclear power plants as used fuel rods totals about 2,000 tons per year. The United States produces a total of about 41 million tons of hazardous waste each year, 8 million tons of which is routinely transported around the country annually. All used nuclear fuel has been managed so that no adverse impacts to human health or the environment has occurred.

*Record of safety.* The nuclear energy industry has carried out more than 2,900 shipments of used nuclear fuel over U.S. highways and railroads since 1964. No nuclear fuel container has ever leaked or cracked in any way. In total, fuel containers were involved in just eight accidents, only four with fuel loaded in the container. The most serious was an overturned truck in 1971. No radiation was released in any of the accidents.

*Fuel container certification.* A nuclear fuel container consists of literally tons of shielding inside a thick steel cylinder. Any container design must be licensed by the U.S. Nuclear Regulatory Commission (NRC) before the container is used for shipment. The NRC will not certify the container until it undergoes a series of rigorous tests demonstrating that it is invulnerable to impact, flames, submersion and puncture.

---

## Radiation Dangers Are Exaggerated

Government officials and scientists keep repeating that any amount of ionizing radiation, no matter how small, must be considered hazardous. This statement is not a scientific truth; in fact, it is contradicted by data from laboratory experiments and epidemiological analysis, and by basic biological theory.

Nevertheless, this statement, and the government policy based on it, are the sole justification for fantastic scenarios of single man-made radioactive atoms migrating for miles, through billions of naturally radioactive atoms in the desert soil, to contaminate water supplies millennia from now.

Such scenarios create needless fear, endless delays, and extraordinary expense. . . . In fact, such waste produces lower exposures to radiation than many naturally radioactive materials in everyday use.

Jim Muckerheide and Ted Rockwell, *Twenty-First Century Science and Technology,* Fall 1997.

---

*Approved transportation routes.* Used nuclear fuel may be shipped only along specified highway routes. Shippers submit routes to the NRC for approval ahead of time. The NRC checks that a route conforms to U.S. Department of Transportation (DOT) regulations, requiring the most direct interstate route, and avoiding large cities when a bypass or beltway is available. NRC officials drive the route ahead of time if it has not been previously approved before or used within the past few years. They will check for law enforcement and emergency response capability as well as secure facilities for emergency stops. DOT regulations also require that the shipper notify the governor of each state on the route seven days before the trip.

*Specialized shippers, certified drivers.* Specialized trucking companies handle used nuclear fuel shipments in the United States. These experienced, specially licensed companies haul all kinds of hazardous materials more than 50 million miles annually. Vehicles are state of the art, equipped with computers that provide an instantaneous update on the truck's location and convey messages between driver and dispatcher through a satellite communications network. Drivers receive extensive training and must be certified.

*Emergency response.* The DOT and NRC establish emergency preparedness requirements for radioactive materials. The Federal Emergency Management Agency and the DOE provide emergency response training for state and local law enforcement officials, fire fighters, and rescue squads, covering preparedness planning and accident handling. In addition, DOE radiological assistance teams provide expertise and equipment, including mobile laboratories, to every region of the country. Also, according to a voluntary mutual assistance agreement, utilities respond to incidents in their area until emergency personnel from the shipper and shipping utility arrive.

## Used Nuclear Fuel: Nonexplosive, Nonflammable

*Used nuclear fuel: ceramic pellets encased in metal tubes.* Used nuclear fuel looks and feels the same as when it was new: a hard ceramic pellet about the size of the tip of your little finger. After 18 to 24 months in the reactor it is less fissionable, that is, less capable of undergoing a nuclear chain reaction. But it is also more radioactive. The metal tubes in which the pellets are inserted when they are manufactured help to contain this radiation. Transportation containers do the rest of the job.

*Used nuclear fuel cannot explode.* Even when new, nuclear fuel is too weak to explode. Uranium mined from the ground is less than 1 percent fissionable and must be enriched to 4 percent in order to be used in a nuclear reactor. The uranium would have to be 20 to 90 percent enriched to be used in a weapon.

*Used nuclear fuel does not burn.* Although people often refer to used nuclear fuel as "nuclear waste," nuclear fuel does not burn when used in a nuclear reactor. In fact, it is not flammable. And, it is not really waste, because it can be recycled to be used in a reactor again; it just needs to be re-enriched.

*Used nuclear fuel is never transported with weapons.* Because used nuclear fuel is so different from weapons-grade uranium, nuclear fuel is never transported with radioactive material from atomic weapons, which, in turn, is never transported by train and never in such a state that it could ever detonate.

"Recycling *[slightly contaminated]* *radioactive material would pose less risk to* *all involved than* disposing *of it."*

# Radioactive Metal Recycling Is Beneficial

S.Y. Chen

S.Y. Chen is leader of the risk assessment and safety evaluation group at the Argonne National Laboratory, a U.S. Department of Energy research institute. In the following viewpoint, Chen argues that recycling slightly radioactive metal from decommissioned nuclear power plants is safer and less costly than disposing of it. Chen asserts that replacing radioactive metal that has been disposed of necessitates the extraction and processing of virgin metals to replace it. This process creates significant environmental and health hazards. In contrast, according to Chen, recycling radioactive metal saves mineral and energy resources, creates less water and air pollution, and produces fewer industrial accidents.

As you read, consider the following questions:
1. According to Chen, what does the term "risk" refer to as used by his risk assessment team?
2. What pathways would radioactive metal take during the recycling process, as stated by Chen?
3. What did Chen's research team conclude was the greatest health risk involved in the handling and processing of radioactive metal?

E very day, most of us take many calculated risks—driving on the expressway, walking across the street, getting on an airplane. Within seconds, we subconsciously weigh and assess the pros and cons of our actions, deciding if the result is worth risking the potential for harm.

## The Risk Assessment Team

A group of researchers at the U.S. Department of Energy's Argonne National Laboratory also spends much of its time weighing risks and consequences—but on a much larger scale.

This multi-disciplinary team of scientists at Argonne, a leading center for risk analysis, has created computer programs to analyze risks to the environment and to human health and safety from such activities as transporting hazardous waste, decommissioning and decontaminating nuclear power plants, and cleanup of weapons production facilities. The researchers use the risk analyses to recommend guidelines for such projects as cleaning up radioactively contaminated materials and sites.

As price tags for environmental site cleanups reach into the hundreds of billions of dollars, the idea of conducting cleanups and setting federal environmental and health regulations based on potential risk is increasingly appealing to lawmakers and regulators. . . .

## Recycling Versus Disposing of Radioactive Material

One example of the value of risk-based analysis is a recent study conducted by Argonne researchers demonstrating at least one instance where *recycling* radioactive material would pose less risk to all involved than *disposing* of it.

At Argonne risk assessment on radioactive metal recycling is a multi-disciplinary effort. It involves scientists in Argonne's Environmental Assessment, Decision and Information Sciences and Reactor Engineering divisions. The results of this study prove that disposing of the slightly contaminated radioactive scrap metals poses twice the risk to humans and the environment as recycling the metal for use in consumer products.

The scrap metal in this study comes from nuclear components and building structures on reactors and other nuclear fuel cycle (mining, extraction, fabrication, etc.) facilities. Unlike the highly radioactive material exposed to the reactor core, the contamination of this scrap metal is very low. The radioactivity levels in general are barely detectable, and the potential exposure on an annual basis would not exceed a fraction of a chest X-ray.

As of 1996, these metals are treated and sent to low-level waste disposal facilities. At a U.S. commercial cost of about $300 per cubic foot, it would cost $40 billion to dispose of the potential worldwide inventory of radioactive scrap metal, which is estimated to be 30 million metric tons. As more nuclear weapons production facilities and commercial nuclear power plants are dismantled, the amount grows of slightly contaminated radioactive scrap metals awaiting treatment and disposal.

The potential scrap value of these metals—$5 billion to $10 billion world-wide—combined with the escalating costs of disposal provides an incentive to find ways to recycle the material.

## Assessing the Risks

Before recycling could be considered an acceptable alternative for handling the radioactive scrap, Argonne researchers had to determine the impacts or risks recycling might pose to workers handling the metal and to consumers who would use products made from it.

The term "risk" refers to a broad spectrum of undesirable consequences, including those that affect human health and safety, the environment, facilities, and measures of economic and social well-being. Examples include personal injury, disease, air and water pollution, and soil contamination. Risk assessment studies evaluate the chances that these undesirable consequences would occur.

Argonne has been assessing risks since the laboratory's beginning 50 years ago, especially the effects of radiation exposure on animals and humans. Over the years, the laboratory's risk capabilities have expanded to include analyzing nuclear power facilities, waste disposal, transport of hazardous waste, and the cleanup of weapons production facilities and other contaminated sites.

Scientists at Argonne analyze risk with sophisticated computer programs, called "environmental pathway analysis models," developed to predict environmental and human health risks of specific actions. They are called pathway analysis models because they let researchers investigate the alternative paths or routes by which exposure can occur. Examples include the sources of risk; the mechanisms by which sensitive human, ecological or other systems become exposed; and the consequences of exposure.

---

## Radioactive Waste Coming Out of Our Ears

The sheer volume of available radioactive metal is astonishing. The U.S. Department of Energy (DOE) "has 3,000 to 4,000 facilities that are in D and D [Decommission and Decontamination] state," says Val Loiselle [Chairman of the Association of Radioactive Metal Recyclers]. "There are 123 commercial nuclear power plants. Thirteen of these are entering the decommissioning pipeline. As these plants come down, we will be seeing lots of metals and equipment."

According to Vince Adams [head of the DOE's National Center for Excellence for Metals Recycle], the DOE's database shows 1,577,000 stockpiled metric tons for both the DOE and the NRC combined.

"And that is dwarfed by what we've got coming," says Jane Powell, program manager of the DOE's metal recycling center. She points to all the metal at the gaseous diffusion plant in Oak Ridge, Tennessee, that was used for the Manhattan Project [which was responsible for creating the first atomic bomb]. That plant now sits idle, awaiting demolition crews. "They have one tunnel there that is a half-mile long," says Powell. "We joke and say you can see the curvature of the earth. You can actually look down and see where the light stops. We are going to have metal coming out of our ears."

Anne-Marie Cusac, *Progressive*, October 1998.

---

Argonne scientists developed families of these models, the most prominent one being RESRAD (RESidual RADioactivity), for the U.S. Department of Energy (DOE) to guide environmental cleanup activities at radioactively contaminated sites. RESRAD is a pathway analysis model that calculates radiation doses and cancer risks to a specific group—

such as workers who handle radioactive materials, or future residents who might establish households on a contaminated site—and suggests criteria for the cleanup of radioactively contaminated soils and building materials. The RESRAD models were extended to also address toxic chemical contaminations as well as ecological risk issues.

The only such model authorized for use by DOE, RESRAD has been used to determine site-specific guidelines for cleanup activities at more than 300 sites in the United States and other countries. A recent survey indicated the analyses using RESRAD contributed to savings in cleanup costs to the federal government of approximately $300 million.

Argonne researchers also developed a set of tools to calculate the risks of transporting radioactive and hazardous materials. These tools are used to analyze the risks to the public and transportation workers under both normal and accident conditions.

## Anatomy of an Assessment

In the project mentioned earlier, DOE commissioned Argonne to estimate the volume and value of the world's radioactive scrap metal. Then researchers were asked to compare the risks of recycling the material with those of sending it to disposal facilities and replacing it with uncontaminated metal.

Using components of the RESRAD model and other existing methods, a team of Argonne researchers—including nuclear, environmental, health risk, and social economics experts—calculated the potential radiological health risks, nonradiological health risks, and environmental and socioeconomic impacts associated with disposing of and recycling the slightly radioactive scrap metal.

Disposing of the scrap metal would require cutting and packaging the metal for transportation and could also involve decontamination to reduce worker exposure and melting to reduce volume.

Disposal also means the loss of the scrap metal from world metal stocks, major portions of which are normally recycled. The discarded metal would be replaced by metal newly produced from ore. Producing new metal involves mining ore, ore enrichment or refining, and metal smelting, as well as producing the energy required for these activities.

Producing new steel also requires coke created from coal for producing iron in steel-making blast furnaces. Emissions from coking ovens can potentially lead to cancers and chronic respiratory ailments.

## Including All Possible Risks

Not all nonradiological risks involved with radioactive scrap metal disposal are derived from production; workplace and transportation accidents were also considered.

To calculate the potential risks of recycling the metal, the Argonne researchers tracked the hypothetical path the metal would take to determine what risks to study. Using computer models, they developed detailed recycling scenarios to assess the potential exposure to workers who would handle the material.

The first step on the recycling path would be to a smelter, where the metal would be melted and made into ingots or slag for use in manufacturing consumer products such as construction materials. The researchers estimated the potential risks to steel workers from exposure to the slightly radioactive metal, as well as the risks to the surrounding community's health, and the environmental impact from smokestack emissions.

The recycled metal would then make its way back to the metal market pool, where it would be used to manufacture major consumer goods such as washers, dryers and automobiles; construction materials; and tools and machinery. Again, using pathway analysis models, the researchers determined the potential risk to both workers and the public from producing these products with recycled radioactive scrap metal.

Along with human health risks, the researchers examined the effects of recycling and disposal on land use and disturbance, water quality and resources, air quality, and mineral and energy resources. Socioeconomic factors were also considered: low-level waste site capacity, public acceptance; metal market impacts, risk distribution, and industrial applications.

The researchers determined that potential health risks in

the form of exposure to radiation and toxic elements, as well as from industrial and transportation accidents, existed for both recycling and disposing of the scrap metal. Under either alternative, regulations would limit radiation exposure of workers and the general public to very low levels.

## A Surprising Conclusion

The highest health risks, however, are those for fatalities or disabling injuries from workplace accidents—and they are higher for the disposal-and-replacement option than for recycling. For recycling, these risks apply to decontamination activities, including controlled smelting and commercial smelting. But the risks are at least twice as high for disposal and replacement, because that option involves iron mining, coal mining, coke production and blast furnace operation in addition to steel smelting.

Recycling is also a more favorable approach environmentally in terms of mineral and energy resource savings and preserving already scarce low-level waste disposal capacity. Recycling the metal generally means 40 percent less water use, 70 percent less energy use, 80 percent less water pollution, 90 percent less air pollution, and 90 percent less raw material use.

Information obtained through risk analysis may prove certain policies or actions beneficial, but it is not the only criterion to be considered when making policy or cleanup decisions.

For example, even though the Argonne researchers concluded that recycling radioactive scrap metal is advantageous in terms of risk, cost, and environmental impact, questions remain regarding public acceptance of recycling the material. In fact, an investigation by Argonne's project team indicated that public acceptance is the biggest single hurdle to recycling radioactive scrap metal. To accept a particular risk, an individual must conclude that the personal benefit outweighs the potential for harm, such as, for example, when someone agrees to have medical or dental X-rays. The benefits of recycling radioactive scrap metal, however, would affect the average citizen only indirectly and are thus harder to accept.

Indeed, the biggest challenge facing both researchers and

lawmakers may be to effectively communicate the concept of risk to the public and to improve public understanding of risk, especially when it involves radioactivity. Public opinion polls show, for example, that many citizens fear exposure to radiation at any level, even though they are exposed to naturally occurring radiation every day, even from their own bodies. Naturally occurring radioactive materials in the human body, such as potassium-40, deliver about two chest X-rays worth of radiation to the average individual each year. Add to that other natural background radiation—such as cosmic rays, terrestrial radiation and radon gas—and most people are exposed to an equivalent of about 30 chest X-rays per year of natural radiation.

Another risk assessment challenge involves answering the question, "How clean is clean?" Standards for certain types of environmental cleanup require levels of radioactivity below naturally occurring levels. Adherence to such strict standards would require extraordinary resources in a time of belt tightening and budget cutting.

Argonne's risk assessment expertise will increasingly be in demand as risk-based decision-making and cost-benefit analysis of environmental laws become standard procedure. The laboratory's researchers are currently using what they have learned in the radioactive scrap metal study to establish recommendations for regulatory guidelines for releasing the scrap metal for recycling. They are also providing risk analysis to DOE on the sale overseas of slightly contaminated nickel.

Other efforts are now underway at Argonne to apply a similar risk-based approach to issues that are of national interest. These include the disposition of mixed waste—a mixture of hazardous chemicals and radioactive materials—and waste from nuclear facility decontamination and decommissioning.

Success of these efforts would mean hundreds of millions of dollars in savings to the Department of Energy in its current waste management operations and environmental cleanup activities. Such savings can be realized without compromising the health and safety of workers and members of the public.

"*It is unclear how the Nuclear Regulatory Commission can reasonably evaluate the human health impacts of [radioactive metal recycling].*"

# Radioactive Metal Recycling Endangers Human Health

David E. Adelman

David E. Adelman is project attorney for the National Resources Defense Council, an environmental organization. In the following statement originally delivered before the Senate Subcommittee on Environment and Public Works, Adelman argues against a standard proposed by the Nuclear Regulatory Commission (NRC) that would permit the unrestricted release of radioactive metal for recycling. Adelman asserts that the government entities charged with regulating nuclear waste have mismanaged nuclear waste in the past and lack the technical capability to accurately measure the risks posed by the recycling of radioactive waste into consumer products. Release standards for radioactive materials are still being debated.

As you read, consider the following questions:
1. According to the author, what basic issues have been raised by the technical constraints on measuring radioactivity?
2. What shortcuts will recycling companies likely take during the processing of radioactive metal in order to maximize profits, as stated by Adelman?

Excerpted from David E. Adelman's statement before the Subcommittee on Clean Air, Private Property, and Nuclear Safety, Senate Committee on Environment and Public Works, March 9, 2000.

The National Resources Defense Council (NRDC) [an environmental organization] opposes the Nuclear Regulatory Commission's (NRC) proposed rule that would permit the unrestricted release of radioactively contaminated materials for use in such things as home appliances, cars, and other consumer products, and that would expose unprotected workers processing contaminated materials at scrap mills to potentially significant levels of radiation. NRDC has fundamental concerns about whether such standards can be implemented safely, particularly in light of the revelations surrounding the Department of Energy's (DOE) Paducah, Kentucky, facility, improper releases of radioactively contaminated materials from DOE's Santa Susana facility in California, and continuing environmental and radiation safety management problems at both private and government facilities generally. Further, NRDC has serious questions about the uncertainties in the estimates of the risks of recycling radioactively contaminated materials to workers and the public. For these reasons, NRDC opposes the NRC's proposed rule and the NRC's current practice of allowing unrestricted releases on a case-by-case basis until these uncertainties are resolved and the NRC has obtained general public acceptance that radioactively contaminated materials can be recycled safely. . . .

## The NRC and DOE Lack Credibility

Public concern about radioactively contaminated materials remains high because of DOE's history of regulatory mismanagement, the technical challenges, and the direct impacts recycling radioactive materials will have on consumer products. Moreover, these concerns have been significantly heightened since the public learned that the major NRC contractor responsible for the technical evaluation of possible standards, Science Applications International Corporation (SAIC), is at the same time working directly for BNFL, Inc., the DOE contractor that is undertaking the first large-scale recycling of radioactively contaminated metals on regulatory compliance issues. This direct conflict of interest has seriously undermined public confidence in the objectivity of the NRC's proposed rulemaking and caused the NRC to initiate an investigation of SAIC and its other contractors on this and other potential conflicts of interest.

NRC therefore must convince a very wary public that it can implement a rule safely, that the underlying science is sound and untainted, and that deregulation is not simply a means of externalizing the decommissioning costs of NRC-licensed and DOE facilities onto the public by recycling radioactive waste into consumer products. Otherwise, the NRC risks creating the backlash it experienced in 1992, when it attempted to deregulate, and causing potentially significant economic harm to the recycling industry, particularly for scrap metals, by burdening it with radioactive wastes that undermine public confidence in recycled products. As the National Research Council ("Council") concluded in a 1996 DOE-commissioned report, public acceptance and understanding are essential.

The 1996 Council study concerned the decommissioning of the DOE's three gaseous diffusion plants. The report included extended analysis of recycling options for the large quantities of scrap metal that would be generated in the decommissioning process. The Council's report included the following recommendations and findings:

- If recycling of scrap metal were to proceed, promulgation of credible national standards for the unrestricted release of radioactively contaminated materials is a necessary prerequisite.
- It is essential that a meaningful stakeholder and public involvement process be implemented before recycling of any radioactively contaminated materials occurs.
- Recycling of contaminated materials could cause significant health risks to workers and the public.
- Great care must be taken to ensure that release of contaminated steel does not increase residual radioactivity in the nation's steel supply to an unacceptable level, particularly because increases in contaminants have been observed in the past.

Despite the absence of accepted standards and any meaningful public involvement, the DOE is proceeding with the first large-scale recycling of contaminated scrap metal at the Oak Ridge K-25 gaseous diffusion plant in Tennessee. In a legal challenge to the DOE's failure to complete an environmental impact statement for the project, federal district court judge Gladys Kessler found:

- that the potential for environmental harm from the Oak Ridge project is great, especially given the unprecedented amount of hazardous materials that would be recycled;
- that DOE should have prepared an environmental impact statement for the Oak Ridge radioactive metals recycling project; and
- that it was "startling and worrisome" that, from an early point on, there was no opportunity for public scrutiny or input on a project of such grave importance.

In addition to the problems identified by Judge Kessler, it appears that under the NRC's regulations the project is proceeding without a valid license. Tennessee lacks the regulatory authority to grant a license where radioactively contaminated materials are recycled for use in consumer products.

The NRC nonetheless supports the Oak Ridge project despite these deficiencies and the present rulemaking it is considering. Moreover, the Oak Ridge project is qualitatively different from prior, more-limited releases because of its scale—approximately 100,000 tons of scrap metal will be recycled—and the types of contaminated materials. The DOE's decision to proceed with the Oak Ridge project, and the NRC's support of it, have further compromised the credibility of the NRC's public participation process. With the Oak Ridge project proceeding under NRC's blessing, public stakeholders question whether a standard is predetermined and whether the proposed NRC rulemaking will fully and fairly consider all of the alternatives, including halting all releases of radioactively contaminated materials. NRDC firmly believes, consistent with the Council's report, that NRC should cease licensing unrestricted releases of radioactively contaminated materials until it resolves these issues and that DOE should also halt all unrestricted releases of radioactive materials from its facilities.

## Serious Implementation Problems

*The total quantity of radioactively contaminated materials to be released for use in commercial products is unknown.*

According to Environmental Protection Agency (EPA) estimates, NRC-licensed facilities contain about 650,000 metric tonnes of scrap metal that could be recycled; however, EPA's upper bound on this estimate is about twice this value. EPA estimates that DOE facilities currently store about 171,000 metric tonnes of scrap metal; although, the upper bound on this estimate is about twice this value. Decommissioning of DOE facilities, according to EPA, will generate approximately another 925,000 tonnes, but the actual quantity could be several times higher than this value. There are no estimates of the total quantities of other radioactive materials (e.g., concrete, soil, industrial wastes) that could be deregulated.

---

## Radioactive Braces

Any exposure to recycled radioactive material, which includes everything from metal to concrete to plastic, could increase the likelihood of cancer, birth defects, reduced immunity, genetic damage, and other negative health effects. If large amounts of this material are sold into the marketplace, your child could be multiply exposed to various radioactive products—from braces to baby strollers. *Exposures to radiation should be avoided and reduced, not legally increased.*

*Public Citizen*, Radioactive Material Recycling FAQ, 2001.

---

Because of these uncertainties, it is unclear how the NRC can reasonably evaluate the human health impacts of its standard. It is essential that the NRC clearly explain how it plans to estimate, in a scientifically sound manner, the total quantity of radioactively contaminated materials to which the public could be exposed, particularly because some radioactive contaminants remain hazardous for many thousands of years. Indeed, several radionuclides such as technetium and uranium have extremely long half-lives, which adds another layer of complexity to NRC's assessment of the aggregate amount of radioactively contaminated materials that will be in commerce at any given time.

The NRC claims that the risks from contaminated metals are limited because contaminated scrap metal will make up less than one percent of the scrap metal being processed in any given year, which would reduce their potential risks. However, this estimate does not take into account scrap mills, particularly mini-mills, that may receive a disproportionate amount of radioactively contaminated metal. At these facilities, recycled metal could be released without being mixed with any clean metal. Under these circumstances, the NRC's claims of significant dilution are merely hypothetical. As in the prior EPA study, the risks from contaminated materials must be evaluated assuming no dilution.

Similarly, because of public concern about aggregate effects of radiation from contaminated materials, it is essential that the NRC provide information on and estimates of exposures from multiple pathways. Under its current analysis the NRC limits its evaluation to certain exposure scenarios without providing adequate information on the broader context of potential exposures. Only with this information will the public be able to assess the relative contributions from different sources and pathways, e.g., the impact of technetium-99 contamination in consumer products relative to that of cobalt-60 or what pathways are most important for each radionuclide. This information should be tabulated and presented in several examples illustrating the effects of different radionuclides in specific circumstances. . . .

*Surveying and monitoring for radioactive contamination is both technically challenging and costly.*

Survey measurements for radioactive contamination are difficult and challenging where large, complicated pieces of equipment, such as that found at DOE and NRC facilities, are involved. Problems that can undermine effective surveying include the following:

Complex geometries with difficult to reach surfaces are challenging to measure accurately, and workers will tend to avoid these measurement areas.

Large errors can be introduced into measurements of volumetric contamination if the contaminant concentration is not uniform or if the geometry of the contaminated piece is complicated.

Even where measurements are straightforward, the accuracy of the measurements is limited by the presence of unavoidable background radiation.

Typical measurement uncertainties, even for the most favorable geometries, are likely to be several percent; more complex geometries will result in greater measurement uncertainty. In its study, EPA acknowledges that current detection instruments may not be sensitive enough to detect contamination reliably under a 1 mrem/y standard, which is a "reasonable" level often quoted by regulators. For example Cobalt-60, a major contaminant in materials at NRC-licensed facilities and an important radionuclide in risk assessments, could be difficult to detect under a 1 mrem/y standard. If a standard is set, the NRC must be able to demonstrate that the available detection equipment can reliably survey materials to satisfy its standard. Conversely, if NRC identifies an acceptable standard but adequate detection equipment is not available for certain radionuclides, unrestricted release of materials contaminated with those radionuclides should be prohibited.

These technical constraints raise several basic issues:

- It is unclear whether the detection equipment available can protect the public against improper releases of radioactively contaminated materials if a stringent standard were set.
- No data have been provided estimating the rate of potential false negatives (measurements that incorrectly find that a piece of equipment is not contaminated).
- NRC has not conducted any assessments of the potential impacts of improper releases on workers or the public.
- NRC has not demonstrated that surveying can be conducted adequately for the large quantities of scrap metal available for recycling at NRC-licensed and DOE facilities. . . .

*The economics of radioactive materials recycling will undermine safe implementation of a standard.*

Except in the case of nickel, and to a lesser extent copper, the primary economic gain from recycling scrap metal and other radioactively contaminated materials derives from avoiding disposal costs. This means that from an economic perspective there is little difference between limiting standards to restricted releases, such as used solely within DOE or NRC-licensed facilities, versus permitting unrestricted recycling of such materials.

However, the savings from avoiding disposal are often more than offset by the costs of cleaning the materials to meet unrestricted release standards and, to a lesser extent, costs from surveying the materials for radioactive contaminants. Unless there are effective regulatory oversight mechanisms and significant penalties for regulatory violations, companies engaged in recycling will (1) maximize the amount of material they release without cleaning it; and (2) seek to limit survey costs. The economics of the radioactive recycling therefore strongly favor lax implementation of surveying requirements and compliance with release standards. Given the amount of material potentially available, the economic incentives, the limits of survey equipment, and the poor track record of the nuclear industry in managing radioactive materials, issuing an NRC standard could result in substantial quantities of material being released in violation of whatever standard might be set.

As discussed above, the NRC must evaluate the potential impacts from such improper releases and ensure that there are regulatory mechanisms to protect the public against them. It is the practical challenges of implementing a standard that represent the greatest source of public concern, even if a safe standard, in principle, were identified. Further, where the risks—particularly to workers—from improper releases are particularly great, the NRC should limit the scope of the permissible types of releases to foreclose the possibility of serious or chronic risks to workers and the public. . . .

## Public Concern

In addition to the problems raised by the lack of public notice and comment in the Oak Ridge project and the direct conflicts of interest of the NRC's major contractor, the present rulemaking is being developed in the context of decades of mismanagement of radioactive wastes at DOE facilities. DOE mismanagement has caused incalculable environmental harm, threatened the health, and in some cases lives, of many DOE workers and U.S. citizens, and created an environmental debacle that will cost more than $250 billion dollars to remedy. Unfortunately, these problems are not merely historical artifacts:

- In 1994, the Conference of Radiation Control Program Directors (CRCPD) found that "[r]adioactive materials have been tracked offsite, into homes, businesses, and elsewhere . . . . States have surveyed people, homes, businesses, rental cars, and trucks. Significant contamination events continue to occur at the DOE facilities due to lack of adequate health physics for all its operations."
- In 1999, the regulatory deficiencies identified by the CRCPD were found at DOE's Paducah, Kentucky, plant, as well as evidence that DOE contractors had illegally disposed of radioactive materials in local sanitary landfills, at random sites in a local state wildlife preserve, and through largely unmonitored on-site recycling operations.
- In 2000 the Los Alamos [New Mexico], Livermore [California], and Savannah River [Georgia] sites have been cited by DOE or the Defense Nuclear Safety Board for regulatory compliance violations.
- In January 2000 at DOE's Santa Susana Field Laboratory just outside Los Angeles, EPA discovered that DOE had illegally released radioactively contaminated wastes for disposal at municipal dumps, sold and recycled radioactively contaminated metals, and sent contaminated trailers to local schools without even conducting adequate monitoring.
- In February 2000, a major radioactivity leak occurred at Indian Point nuclear plant in New York.

## Undermined Confidence

These continuing problems undermine public confidence in either DOE's or NRC's ability to ensure that radioactively contaminated materials are managed safely. Moreover, in the wake of the Paducah findings, it is disturbing to consider that the Oak Ridge field office, which also has authority over the Paducah plant, is responsible for overseeing the Oak Ridge radioactive metals recycling project. . . .

The NRC's proposed rulemaking will directly affect the ability of DOE and its contractors to release radioactively contaminated materials, which DOE has time and again failed to manage safely even in a fully regulated environment. In the absence of significant changes within DOE or, at the very least, independent regulatory mechanisms to ensure that radioactive materials are properly managed by DOE, the public has little reason to believe that free releases from DOE facilities, which contain the bulk of the inventory, will occur without serious adverse impacts. It is therefore essential that the NRC consider the practical, technical, and administrative limitations of the entities that will be responsible for releasing contaminated materials into U.S. markets, and that it factor these constraints into its decision on how to proceed.

In the absence of fundamental changes, the NRC should not proceed with this rulemaking, and the NRC and DOE should impose a moratorium on the unrestricted recycling and sale of radioactively contaminated materials for use in, among other things, consumer products until these issues are resolved and public confidence is restored.

> "*Advancements in wastewater and biosolids treatment technologies . . . have improved the quality of biosolids, allowing local governments to develop beneficial uses for sludge [such as fertilizer].*"

# Recycling Sewer Sludge into Fertilizer Is Beneficial

Lori Irvine and Anne Bonelli

Lori Irvine and Anne Bonelli contend in the following viewpoint that properly treated sewer sludge—called biosolids—can be processed into different types of fertilizer. Recent technological advancements and increasingly stringent environmental laws have made recycling sludge less costly than disposing of it, according to the authors. Cities can make money selling the fertilizer for use on lawns, forests, and croplands. Lori Irvine and Anne Bonelli write for *American City and County* magazine, which serves city and county officials who are charged with implementing local government projects.

As you read, consider the following questions:
1. According to the authors, to what does the EPA attribute the growth in biosolids recycling?
2. How has DeKalb County, Georgia, benefited from biosolids recycling, as related by Irvine and Bonelli?
3. What strategies do the authors recommend to educate the public about the benefits of recycling sludge?

Facing limitations on traditional means of biosolids disposal, local governments are finding safe and beneficial ways to recycle their sludge.

In the last 15 years, the federal government has passed legislation regulating biosolids management, limiting traditional methods of disposal—incineration, landfilling and ocean dumping—and making them more expensive than they once were. For example, the 1988 Ocean Dumping Ban Act, the Part 503 Biosolids Rule, and the Part 258 Landfill Rule address, among other things, biosolids disposal and its effect on the environment.

As a result of regulatory changes, cities and counties are increasingly opting to recycle sludge rather than dispose of it. In particular, land application is proving to be an option of growing interest for local governments.

## Beneficial Changes

Since the enactment of the Clean Water Act in 1972, the amount of municipal biosolids produced annually has nearly doubled. According to the U.S. Environmental Protection Agency (EPA), municipalities will produce an estimated 7 million dry tons of sludge in 2000, compared to more than 4.5 million dry tons in 1972. (The increase is attributed mainly to population growth.) EPA projects that, by 2010, U.S. cities will produce more than 8 million dry tons of sludge annually.

Prior to the passage of regulations limiting the number of pollutants and pathogens in biosolids, most of the sludge generated in the United States was disposed of in landfills. However, advancements in wastewater and biosolids treatment technologies—including wastewater pretreatment and pollution prevention programs—have improved the quality of biosolids, allowing local governments to develop beneficial uses for sludge.

The method by which biosolids are beneficially used depends largely on what is cost-effective for the community. According to Bob Brobst, biosolids coordinator for EPA Region 8 and manager of EPA's Biosolids Data Management System, 50 to 60 percent of the biosolids produced today are applied to land as fertilizer or as a soil additive, up from 33 percent in 1988. "Land application has nearly doubled in 12 years, and I don't see that changing," he says.

EPA also credits federal and state regulations and guidance—in particular the Part 503 Biosolids Rule—for nearly eliminating the disposal of biosolids in landfills and for encouraging biosolids recycling. EPA attributes the growth in biosolids recycling to public outreach and marketing; the high cost of biosolids disposal in some locations; disposal bans in some landfills; landfill capacity concerns; landfill closures; and additional research into the safe, beneficial use of biosolids.

Nevertheless, in some areas of the country, biosolids recycling is decreasing as local governments take advantage of low landfill costs. EPA is unsure whether those areas will affect the overall trend away from biosolids disposal.

## Land Applications

Land application, which has been practiced for decades, involves spreading biosolids on the soil surface. When properly treated and processed, biosolids enrich soil and can supplement or even replace commercial fertilizers.

Historically, biosolids have been applied to agricultural crops, forests, parks and golf courses, and used in the reclamation of mines and other drastically disturbed sites. Composted and treated biosolids are used frequently by landscapers and nurseries and by homeowners for lawns and home gardens.

DeKalb County, Georgia, is one of many local governments that have implemented a land application program for biosolids reuse. In 1991, as the county planned a wastewater treatment plant expansion, officials began looking for economic and environmentally responsible ways to recycle the biosolids.

The expansion included the addition of an advanced secondary treatment facility capable of treating 20 million gallons of wastewater per day. The plant currently produces 8,888 pounds of Class B dry solids [which may contain pathogens] each day, and the county applies it to a 550-acre hay field adjacent to the treatment facility.

The field produces 300 to 600 pounds of Bermuda hay

per acre per year. Beef cattle, horses, mules, goats and even the elephants at Zoo Atlanta have benefited from the 12,926 tons of hay harvested during the past nine years. Additionally, by implementing the land application program, the county has saved more than 129,000 yards of landfill space.

Similarly, Taos, New Mexico, has saved landfill space by producing and selling pelletized biosolids for use as fertilizer. For years, the town had used lime to stabilize sludge and then applied it to a disposal site behind the treatment plant. However, in 1998, Taos was running out of land on which to dispose of the sludge, and the only remaining, affordable parcel was situated on the outskirts of town. The dilemma: either truck the biosolids through neighborhoods, angering the homeowners, or haul the sludge to the local landfill, which was quickly running out of space.

In the end, the town vetoed both options and turned instead to Biosolids Enrichment and Recycling (BER). The process takes dewatered sludge into a continuous flow process where it reacts in an enclosed environment with ammonia, acid and potassium, rendering the biosolids sterile and stable. The process produces Class A quality fertilizer [which contains no disease-causing organisms].

By using the BER process, Taos has eliminated the need for lime stabilization, land application and permitting. The biosolids are sold in pellet form to farms, allowing the town to recover some of the costs of the treatment process and return the biosolids to the soil, where air and water break down the organic material.

## Import, Export

In states such as New York and Massachusetts, where open space is nearly nonexistent and the distance to agricultural land is substantial, land application is largely out of the question. In those states, communities are hauling their biosolids to other states, where there is opportunity for reuse. For example, dewatered Class B cake biosolids from New York City and Class A pelletized biosolids from Boston fertilize land in Prowers County, Colorado.

In fact, Colorado has the largest interstate land application program in the country. In 1998, 12,715 wet tons of biosolids were applied to land, and, in 1999, 36,875 wet tons were applied—covering nearly 40,000 acres in Prowers County. About 75 percent of that is applied to dryland winter wheat, while the remainder is used on rangeland, sand dunes, irrigated alfalfa and irrigated corn.

By involving the regional health department in the project, Parker Ag Services, the Limon, Colorado-based company that operates the project, has been able to build public support for importing biosolids. In each community that receives sludge, the regional health department monitors the process and oversees the land application program to ensure that it is being operated properly. "An informed and educated community is critical to the success of any land application program—especially one that transports biosolids two-thirds of the way across the United States," says Mike Sharp, director of program development for the operating company.

---

## An Ancient Practice

Recycling human waste has a long and noble history. Chinese agriculture, for example, was sustained for thousands of years by the "night soil" collected from cities and rural villages. In his classic study *Farmers of Forty Centuries*, agricultural historian F.H. King reports that farmers would build roadside outhouses and post advertising to entice travelers to use them, so desired was the excrement as a supplemental source of nutrients and organic matter.

Gary Gardner, *World Watch*, January/February 1998.

---

Ultimately, the public's perception of the safety and value of biosolids recycling will have a major impact on a community's ability to market biosolids usage and products. Many current programs—including that in Prowers County—would not be successful without public buy-in.

To overcome public resistance to biosolids reuse, local governments must include education in their beneficial use strategies. For example, they should hold town meetings, conduct open houses, work with the media and provide the public with information resources.

According to EPA, of the 7 million tons of biosolids generated in 1998, 60 percent was beneficially used (land applied, composted, used as landfill cover), and the rest was disposed of with no attempt to recover nutrients or other valuable properties. EPA estimates that, in 2000, 63 percent of the biosolids generated will be beneficially used, and it expects growth in biosolids recycling to continue. In fact, the agency is estimating that 70 percent of all biosolids produced in 2010 will be beneficially used.

Part of that growth will depend on the development of new technologies. For example, technologies exist that can transform organic waste to raw materials for industrial use. Many processes are advancing from the pilot test stage and nearing commercial use.

Additionally, growing acceptance of beneficial use of biosolids could lead to increasing biosolids recovery in the future. Effective public outreach and educational programs may make biosolids usage as acceptable as recycling the daily newspaper and soft drink cans.

*"There is plenty of documentary evidence that sludge can be dangerous to people and other living things."*

# Recycling Sewer Sludge into Fertilizer Is Harmful

Sheila R. Cherry

Sheila R. Cherry argues in the following viewpoint that the recycling of sewer sludge into fertilizer endangers the health of people working in wastewater treatment plants and living near land where the fertilizer is applied. Children have died from exposure to recycled sludge, she contends, and numerous other people have grown seriously ill. Cherry claims that the U.S. Environmental Protection Agency fails to adequately oversee the recycling of sewer sludge and misleads the public about its dangers. Sheila R. Cherry writes for *Insight on the News* magazine.

As you read, consider the following questions:

1. According to Cherry, what health problems have residents of Osceola Mills experienced since recycled sewer sludge was applied to a mine-reclamation site near their town?
2. What recommendations did government officials make to minimize the health risk posed by recycling sewer sludge at the LeSourdsville, Ohio, wastewater treatment plant?
3. Why did a Greenland, New Hampshire, hunter stop hunting deer?

The Environmental Protection Agency (EPA) allows sewer sludge to be recycled and used as fertilizer to grow food. But many say the sludge causes illness and even death.

## The "S" Word

Muddy fields are irresistible to boys, especially boys with motorcycles. Tony Behun, whose elementary-school principal recalls him as a "super kid" whom everybody liked, was no exception. At age 11 he lived just outside the sleepy hamlet of Osceola Mills, Pennsylvania—its population in 1996 was 1,282. And Tony was oblivious to the pathogens he was churning up when he spent an afternoon in 1994 racing his mom, Brenda, on her three-wheel all-terrain vehicle through the fresh mud at the coal-mine quarry a half-mile uphill from his home.

Only it wasn't mud. It was sewer sludge—a by-product from chemically treated human waste, which the Environmental Protection Agency insists is safe to recycle as fertilizer.

The EPA doesn't like using the "s" word: sludge. So it hired the Washington public-relations firm of Powell Tate to find a more commodious term. Powell Tate's wordsmiths coined the environment-friendly phrase "biosolids." In a memo, Robert Perciasepe, then the EPA's Office of Water assistant administrator, enlisted EPA employees in the campaign to win public acceptance. "Your use of the word 'biosolids' is an important component in accomplishing one of EPA's policy objectives—supporting and encouraging the beneficial use of these residuals of wastewater treatment."

## Play Turned Deadly

Whatever it was called, biosolids were not all that beneficial for young Tony. Racing through a fresh mound of what he thought was dirt at the quarry that Wednesday evening in October seemed natural-enough fun to the 11-year-old. Without "no trespassing" or warning signs to discourage access to the mine-reclamation site, it was just another muddy field to attract a country kid with a bike. But the following day Tony began complaining of a sore throat and a headache. The symptoms worsened on the second day, when his mom, Brenda Behun Robertson, noticed that boils had developed on Tony's left arm and leg.

Soon the boy developed flulike symptoms, prompting Robertson to call the family doctor, who prescribed an antibiotic. The symptoms worsened the following day and Tony began to have trouble breathing. That evening he was rushed to a hospital emergency room.

Tony's degenerating condition puzzled the doctors, who ordered him airlifted to Allegheny General Hospital, where more-extensive tests could be performed. Brenda says the doctors "did everything possible but could neither improve nor diagnose Tony's illness." The next morning—on Oct. 21, eight days after exposure to the sludge-treated ground at the reclamation site—Tony Behun was dead.

And there is more: Rare cancers reportedly are common in tiny Osceola Mills. A school official has an inflammatory breast cancer of a kind rarely seen. A second-grader has leukemia. A fourth-grader has another rare cancer. The general increase in cancer diagnoses has created alarm. Robertson and her husband tell *Insight* that almost every family they know in the area has someone who has contracted cancer. And, of course, their Tony is dead.

## Sludge Safety

The EPA says its mission is "to protect human health and to safeguard the natural environment—air, water and land—upon which life depends." It issued "Standards for the Use or Disposal of Sewage Sludge" regulations, or "Part 503," in 1993. Since then, the EPA has insisted that biosolids are good for us—"nutrient-rich" and "primarily organic." On an EPA public-information Website, officials of the agency proclaim: "Biosolids recycling is safe and the food crops grown on land fertilized with biosolids are safe to eat."

But sludge comes in two forms based on the level of pathogens that are detected in it. Pathogens, says the EPA, are disease-causing organisms such as certain bacteria and viruses.

After being treated to a point where the organisms cannot be readily detected, sludge is graded Class A "exceptional quality." Class A, or "EQ" sludge, is treated as any other fertilizer and even has been sold commercially for lawns and home gardens.

But bacteria and viruses can be detected in Class B sludge, according to the National Institute for Occupational Safety and Health, or NIOSH, though it has been reduced to concentrations "that are unlikely to pose a health risk to the public and the environment." Even so, Class B sludge is intended only for use where it will have little exposure to humans. Land to which it has been applied is supposed to be restricted from high-traffic public access for at least one year. Even low-trafficked land is supposed to be restricted from public access for 30 days after sludge has been applied.

Waste-management companies are paid $40 to $75 a ton to dispose of sewer sludge produced by water-treatment plants. The companies offer it to landowners as a low-cost or free fertilizer in exchange for permission to dump it. Former strip-mine sites and rural farms frequently are used. Permit documents indicate that landowners are under no specific obligation to post signs warning the public that potentially hazardous sewage has been dumped as sludge on their property. Transport documents indicate one former mine site received in excess of 5,000 tons of sludge within a one-month period.

According to the Maryland-based waste-management company BioGro, Inc., "Besides improving soil, land-applied biosolids supplement or replace commercial fertilizer. This means farmers save money." BioGro promotes biosolids as ideal for reclaiming strip-mined land and increasing timber production in forest land. "One city [Milwaukee] uses its biosolids to make a popular lawn and turf fertilizer sought throughout the U.S.," the company's Website states. But BioGro frequently has been cited in complaints about sludge dumping, and doubts persist. Public outcry in 1998 prompted the Department of Agriculture, or USDA, to refuse to allow crops grown in biosolid fertilizer to be labeled "organic."

A press release from the waste-management industry association, the Water Environment Federation, or WEF, says such labeling is based on marketing, not science. "The basis for the exclusion of biosolids amounts to no more than a 'beauty contest' due to the lack of scientific justification." Nevertheless, after receiving "an unprecedented 275,603 comments during the first go around" concerning use of biosolids as fertilizer for organic foods, Agriculture Secretary Dan Glickman reaffirmed his opposition in March 2000. "As I've stated before, in no case will the use of irradiation, sewer sludge or genetic engineering be permitted in the production of any organic foods or ingredients."

The WEF doesn't win them all, but it provides advice to local government officials about stonewalling citizen and media inquiries. For example, in its "Guidelines for Releasing Information," WEF advises municipal officials: "U.S. government agencies must follow the Freedom of Information Act for guidance on information that must be released. But you, as a local government entity, do not have to follow this law."

## Lax Oversight

The WEF and EPA, meanwhile, stop just short of calling biosolids delicious, declaring land-applied sludge safe due to "site restrictions and good management practices" that are required for processing those Class B biosolids that EPA itself says may contain pathogens. What about regulatory oversight: Is Congress protecting public health? Not so, says the EPA's Office of Inspector General, or OIG.

While testifying before the House Science Committee in March, EPA Office of Water Assistant Administrator J. Charles Fox discussed the OIG's final audit report on the EPA's treatment of biosolids, which had been issued just two days earlier. Committee spokesman Jeff Lungren [explains] that Fox's disclosure surprised the committee's staffers, who were unaware such a report existed. The disclosure sent them scrambling to track down a copy even as the hearing was taking place.

"It doesn't exactly inspire confidence that you're getting the full facts" when things like that happen, says Lungren. "We were very interested in what it had to say."

What the audit report said was that EPA oversight of waste-management practices beyond site inspections at water-treatment facilities virtually was nonexistent. Officials in the OIG reported: "EPA does not have an effective program for ensuring compliance with the land-application requirements of Part 503. Accordingly, while the EPA promotes land application, EPA cannot assure the public that current land-application practices [for biosolids] are protective of human health and the environment."

The EPA's own State Sludge Management Program Guidance Manual indicates that enforcement of land application of sludge is passive. Included in the manual is a memo from Michael Cook, director of the EPA's Office of Wastewater Enforcement and Compliance, to regional water-management division directors regarding the "National Approach to Sewage Sludge Implementation." According to Cook: "As we have previously agreed, the primary emphasis of our compliance and enforcement activities will be directed toward Class I Sludge Management Facilities," not the EPA-encouraged spreading of biosolids on the land.

## Public Concern

Tony Behun's neighbors brought their concerns about the spreading of sludge to the attention of the EPA and the Department of Environmental Protection, or DEP. They say they were ignored and treated as NIMBYs—people with a Not-In-My-Back-Yard resistance to sludge-dumping in their town.

John Walker of the EPA's Office of Environmental Management Systems for Biosolids defends the spreading of biosolids but admits the response to problems "is not where we'd like it to be." Asked if land-applied sludge is a benign issue, Walker responds, "I think so; I think some people don't think so." He says "it is inherently built into some people's perceptions that if something smells bad, it's got to be hazardous." But he says biosolids can be very beneficial even as a preventive agent for lead poisoning.

"You can take Class A biosolids around old homes high in lead paint and mix it into the soil." Not only will the nutrients in the sludge thicken the lawn cover above the ground where the paint fragments settle, according to Walker, the biosolid material forms a chemical "tie" with the lead-paint fragments. "So if a child ingests [lead paint mixed with biosolids] they would be more protected" than ingesting lead-paint fragments alone.

Brenda Robertson admits she long was unaware that

sludge was a possible cause for her son's death. Tony's body was not autopsied. But, without contacting or informing the family, DEP officials conducted an investigation of the boy's death and concluded he died of a bacterial infection—but asserted the infection was contracted from a bee sting received before the sludge was spread. The mother categorically denies Tony was stung by a bee. She found out about the DEP study only by reading a newspaper account in 1999.

## More Illness

By now, the residents of Osceola Mills were not the only ones who were outraged and complaining about an EPA cover-up. In a December 1999 letter John Acey, president of the local United Mine Workers union in Cincinnati, reported that several workers in Centre County, Pa., had experienced symptoms ranging from burning eyes and sore throats to nausea and bloody vomit after being exposed to Class B sludge that was spread "within feet of their work area and haul road." Acey told Nancy Burton of NIOSH that the men's symptoms were very similar to organic amine toxic-gas exposure. He also requested that possible exposure to toxic gas be included in the investigation.

---

### Radioactive Fertilizer

The use of industrial toxic waste as a fertilizer ingredient is a growing national phenomenon. In Gore, Oklahoma, a uranium-processing plant is getting rid of low-level radioactive waste by licensing it as a liquid fertilizer and spraying it over nine thousand acres of grazing land. In Tifton County, Georgia, more than a thousand acres of peanut crops were wiped out by a brew of hazardous waste and limestone sold to unsuspecting farmers. And in southwest Washington highly corrosive, lead-laced waste from a pulp mill is hauled to nearby farms and spread over crops grown for livestock consumption.

Duff Wilson, *Amicus Journal*, Spring 1998.

---

Burton's response three months later was that no bacteria pathogens related to gastrointestinal illness were detected in the sludge samples collected, "indicating there was no residual biological activity specifically related to the sewage sludge." The bacteria that investigators found "are associated with outdoor environments," she said. In reply to the request for air-toxicity tests, Burton stated, "If additional bio-solids occur in the spring of 2000, we intend to conduct bioaerosol monitoring. . . ."

In 1998, NIOSH officials had been requested to evaluate a wastewater treatment plant in LeSourdsville, Ohio, when five workers there reported gastrointestinal illnesses including headaches, diarrhea and abdominal cramping, after working with Class B biosolids at the site. In that NIOSH evaluation, officials confirmed that bacteria that was detected in both air and sludge samples posed the "potential for sewage workers to be occupationally exposed to organisms which have been associated with gastrointestinal symptoms/illnesses."

The recommendations offered by NIOSH officials to minimize worker exposure included hand-washing, protective clothing and inoculations, cleaning vehicles and retrofitting them with clean-air devices, guidance on the proper storage of sludge and "periodic training regarding standard hygiene."

In describing how sludge is applied to land, the NIOSH report noted, "The sludge-spreader operator sprays sludge on the field and, usually, a separate tractor operator disks it into the soil."

## "God's Little Acre"

Symptoms like those experienced by the Pennsylvania and Ohio workers were markedly similar to those that proved fatal for 26-year-old Shayne Conner from the town of Greenland, N.H., which his mother calls "God's little acre." Shayne's family was unable to talk about the circumstances surrounding his death because of a pending legal action with Bio-Gro. However, public statements his mother made before the legal action give a clear indication of the desperate fight she waged to save her son's life.

At a March 1999 press conference at the National Press Club, Joanne Marshall, Shayne's mother, said that in mid-October 1995, tractor-trailer haulers began trucking load after load of sludge through her neighborhood and dumping it on a field next door. The overpowering stench, she said, made her and her neighbors virtual prisoners in their homes. Too much exposure to the air outside caused nausea, vomiting, headaches and stomach cramps. "As days and weeks went by," Marshall reported in a statement, "we became sicker and sicker."

Calling the police did not help; neither did their pleas to the chairman of the local selectmen. The woman who owned the field where the sludge was being spread apologized for the smell but told her neighbors that she had been assured the material was harmless. On the eve of Thanksgiving, one month later, Marshall was awakened by the screams of Shayne's brother, who had discovered Shayne unconscious and gasping for air. The family called 911, but Shayne died at the hospital.

Marshall's torment did not end there. She immediately found herself in another desperate battle to save her small daughter. The sleepless nights before the girl recovered were spent trying to help the child cough up thick mucous and fight off viruses. "Trips to the doctors and hospital emergency rooms became a frequent thing for my neighbors and us," says a Marshall statement.

Some of the adults in the neighborhood developed abscesses and cysts; allergenic illnesses were discovered in the babies; men suffered severe nosebleeds; children complained of unbearable migraine headaches. Marshall and her neighbors had tumor masses surgically removed from their breasts. "The list goes on and on," according to the statement. Hunters in Osceola Mills say they have noticed tumors in game animals. One hunter recited his rule, "What I don't eat, I don't hunt." Since the tumors have started developing in the local deer, he says, he has stopped hunting for fear of eating diseased meat.

Throughout the ordeal over sludge application, the stock EPA and local DEP response has been that there is "no documented evidence" that sludge is not safe. Government whistle-blowers, community activists and victims report they have been subjected to obstruction, misinformation and intimidation.

Never mind that there is plenty of documentary evidence that sludge can be dangerous to people and other living things. Former EPA microbiologist David Lewis has written many articles detailing health risks associated with exposure to Class B sludge. According to Lewis, "Exposure to sufficiently high concentrations of gaseous organic amines can cause severe irritation of the eyes and skin and damage to mucus membranes leading to pulmonary edema [bleeding in the respiratory system]. These toxic gases can also cause damage to the lungs, liver and other internal organs."

Researchers at the Waste Management Institute at Cornell University question the scientific methodology on which EPA officials are basing their safety assurances. In their thesis, The Case for Caution, Cornell researchers Ellen Harrison, Murray McBride and David Bouldin warn that EPA's land-application standards for sewage sludge "were developed through an extensive risk assessment, but data gaps and non-protective policy choices result in regulations which are not adequately protective of human health and the environment."

The victims of these policies say that the EPA has gotten behind a sludge program allegedly to protect the environment and, when people began to sicken and die, became as intransigent as any other accused polluter.

# Periodical Bibliography

The following articles have been selected to supplement the diverse views presented in this chapter.

| | |
|---|---|
| Luther J. Carter | "It's Time to Lay This Waste to Rest," *Bulletin of the Atomic Scientists*, January/February 1997. |
| Sheila R. Cherry | "EPA's Secret Role in Toxic Sludge," *Insight on the News*, July 24, 2000. |
| Mitchell Cohen and Brooklyn Greens | "Toxic Waste and the New World Order," *Synthesis/Regeneration*, Fall 2000. |
| Anne-Marie Cusac | "Nuclear Spoons: Hot Metal May Find Its Way to Your Dinner Table," *Progressive*, October 1998. |
| James DeLong | "Inadequate Superfund Reform," *Regulation*, Spring 1997. |
| *Fertilizer International* | "A Groundless Fear?" January/February 1998. |
| Richard A. Kerr | "Radioactive Waste Disposal: For Radioactive Waste from Weapons, a Home at Last," *Science*, March 12, 1998. |
| Loren McArthur and Marc Beslow | "Polluters and Politics," *Dollars and Sense*, July 17, 1998. |
| Jim Motavelli | "Toxic Targets: Polluters That Dump on Communities of Color Are Finally Being Brought to Justice," *E Magazine*, July 17, 1998. |
| Pat Phibbs | "Who's in Charge of Nuclear Waste?" *World & I*, May 1, 1998. |
| Katherine Probst and Adam Lowe | "The $200 Billion Question: Does Anyone Care About Cleaning Up the Nation's Nuclear Weapons Sites?" *Resources*, Winter 2000. |
| Michael A. Rivlin | "The Superstress of Superfund," *Amicus Journal*, Winter 1999. |
| Linda Rothstein | "Explosive Secrets," *Bulletin of the Atomic Scientists*, March 1, 1999. |
| Karen B. Wiley and Steven L. Rhodes | "From Weapons to Wildlife: The Transformation of the Rocky Mountain Arsenal," *Environment*, June 1, 1998. |
| Jim Wilson | "Putting Nuclear Waste to Work," *Popular Mechanics*, June 1, 1998. |

# CHAPTER 4

# What Innovations Will Help Reduce Waste?

# Chapter Preface

New technologies are enabling cities to solve garbage problems while at the same time addressing energy scarcity. One innovation allows cities to burn residential, commercial, and institutional waste—called municipal solid waste, or MSW—in order to generate electricity. These waste-to-energy facilities use the heat from combustion to produce steam and generate electricity that can then be used to power homes and businesses. By burying the ash produced by incineration rather than the waste itself, cities can reduce the amount of garbage being disposed of in landfills. According to the Baseline Institute at Pace University in New York, these waste-to-energy facilities "can generate energy while reducing the volume of waste by up to 90 percent." Fortunately, modern incinerators are equipped with better emission controls and can burn MSW without emitting as many harmful pollutants as older plants did.

Another way to simultaneously solve garbage and energy problems is to use landfill gas as fuel. As the garbage in landfills decomposes, it creates methane and varying amounts of other gases. Improperly released methane gas can pollute the air, a major concern of those living near landfills. However, cities can now build power plants near landfills that generate electricity by burning this dangerous gas. Gas-to-energy generators release only about 5 percent of the methane that would rise into the air from the landfill itself. As of 2001, only 240 of the 6,000 landfills across the United States had gas-to-energy plants in operation, but the U.S. Environmental Protection Agency estimates that up to 700 more landfills could be equipped to convert methane into energy.

Plants that turn garbage problems into energy solutions are popular with many city officials and environmentalists. The authors in the following chapter discuss other innovations that can help reduce waste. Although people often create environmental problems, they are also quite ingenious when it comes to solving them.

"*[The medical] pollution prevention campaign . . . has . . . motivated countless hospitals to conduct waste audits and establish recycling programs, and catalyzed the use of replacements for toxic materials used in medical devices.*"

# Strategies to Minimize Medical Pollution Can Reduce Toxic Waste

Charlie Cray

In the following viewpoint, Charlie Cray explains that an organization of health care workers and environmentalists has succeeded in forcing hospitals to reduce medical pollution. Cray reports that under the organization's pressure, fewer hospitals are incinerating medical waste, which creates toxins harmful to human health. The organization has also convinced numerous hospitals to curtail the use of mercury thermometers and PVC medical devices such as IV bags, which pollute the environment when disposed of. Charlie Cray is associate editor for the *Multinational Monitor*, a monthly magazine.

As you read, consider the following questions:

1. According to Cray, how was the HCWH able to convince hospitals to stop incinerating medical waste?
2. Why did Jamie Harvie think mercury thermometers were a good issue with which to lead the campaign against medical pollution, as related by the author?
3. As stated by Cray, what risks to human health are posed by the use of PVC medical devices?

Excerpted from "Taking on Toxics II: Health Care Without Harm," by Charlie Cray, *Multinational Monitor*, January/February 2001. Copyright © 2001 by *Multinational Monitor*. Reprinted with permission.

Environmental and public health activists were astonished to discover in the mid-1990s that U.S. Environmental Protection Agency (EPA) analysis showed that medical waste incinerators were the biggest source of dioxin in the United States.

## Do No Harm?

"The irony that the health care industry should be the leading source of one of the most toxic substances around seemed extremely compelling," says Charlotte Brody, a registered nurse and organizer with the Center for Health, Environment and Justice. "It was an extraordinary organizing opportunity because we knew that most health care professionals who knew about the issue would want to do something about it."

Soon Brody and others from 28 organizations—a core of environmental activists, nurses, doctors and public health advocates—formed Health Care Without Harm (HCWH), a broad-based campaign designed to reform the environmental practices of the health care industry.

"Health Care Without Harm is driven by the fundamental notion that the health care industry has a particular ethical responsibility to minimize adverse impacts on public health and the environment," says Dr. Ted Schettler, science director of the Science and Environmental Health Network. "The health care industry can play a leadership role by looking beyond regulatory compliance and doing what's necessary to prevent illness rather than working only to treat it after it occurs."

The organization has developed quickly. In just five years, HCWH has grown to represent nearly 300 organizations in over 25 countries, including more than 88 health care institutions, health-affected constituencies (groups representing people afflicted with cancer, endometriosis and other diseases, as well as children's health advocates), associations of health professionals, religious organizations and many local and national environmental organizations.

Organized into various work groups, the campaign has deployed a flexible matrix of strategies to force the health care industry to apply its ethical commitment to "First, Do

No Harm" to the environmental and occupational impacts of the technologies and materials used in health care. The result has been a holistic and sophisticated pollution prevention campaign that has forced the closure of hundreds of medical waste incinerators, motivated countless hospitals to conduct waste audits and establish recycling programs, and catalyzed the use of replacements for toxic materials used in medical devices, such as mercury and polyvinyl chloride plastics (PVC).

## Campaign Origins

Incinerators were HCWH's first target. In addition to supporting local community-based campaigns that have shut down over 20 medical waste incinerators since the campaign began, HCWH has stigmatized incineration in general and moved hospitals and clinics towards waste segregation, recycling and the selection of safer infectious waste treatment methods.

"Working with nurses and others who knew health care institutions from the inside, we often did for the health care industry what EPA wasn't doing through their new incinerator regulations," says Tracey Easthope of the Ecology Center of Ann Arbor, Michigan. "We even provided information demonstrating how waste reduction and alternative treatment technologies could save them money."

While learning to use such carrots, the campaign also wielded a big stick, working to strengthen U.S. EPA's new medical waste incinerator regulations. The stricter emissions standards forced hundreds of additional hospitals to choose between paying to upgrade their facilities with expensive new emissions control equipment or stop burning their waste and seek viable alternatives.

With the help of Essential Action, a project of Essential Information, the publisher of *Multinational Monitor*, the anti-incineration effort has also expanded abroad, to India and other countries where incinerator manufacturers migrated after the U.S. market declined.

In 2001, HCWH released a report that evaluates non-incineration waste treatment technologies appropriate for less industrialized nations.

## Medical Pollution Prevention

Another flank of HCWH's work has been to reduce the use of toxic substances.

"Mercury is a good issue to lead with because there are readily available alternatives for common uses like fever thermometers and because, unlike with PVC, there isn't a huge lobby behind mercury that would bring in a group of people in three-piece suits to harass the agency people when they tried to do something," says Jamie Harvie, a coordinator of the mercury strategy for HCWH.

Soon after HCWH took up the issue, the U.S. EPA and the American Hospital Association entered into a memo of understanding that calls upon hospitals to phase out their use of mercury by 2005. HCWH campaign materials were reported to be key documents in the development of the memo of understanding.

At the same time, to gain real community engagement of the issue, local HCWH members organized thermometer "swaps" and "round-ups" at hospitals, schools and homes.

Thus far, HCWH has gathered mercury-free facility pledges from more than 600 clinics and hospitals.

At first, the pledges were not enough to affect the major retailers of thermometers—including K-Mart, Albertson's, CVS, Wal-Mart and Walgreens—who continued selling mercury thermometers in the face of a growing demand for alternatives.

## Ratcheting Up the Pressure

But HCWH organizers ratcheted up the pressure on the local level in several towns and cities, beginning with Duluth, Minnesota in March 2000, followed by San Francisco, Ann Arbor and Boston, where laws were passed banning the sale of mercury fever thermometers.

The ordinances had an extraordinary effect. The governor of Massachusetts, for instance, called upon other communities to follow Boston's example the day after its ordinance passed, and the administrator of EPA's New England region recommended that other states follow suit.

"Most retailers order their thermometers in one big batch," Jamie Harvie explains. "I think they were scared that they'd be stuck with what was essentially an illegal product in a few local places, so they decided to switch company-wide. This demonstrates once again the power of local organizing."

The strategy also demonstrated the power of HCWH's holistic approach, which allows the campaign to emphasize either the environmental or human health angle, depending upon the audience and circumstance.

By carefully integrating both environmental and occupational health concerns, HCWH also ensures that what are considered acceptable alternatives to existing practices "doesn't shift the risk between occupational exposures and the environment," says Susan Wilburn of the American Nurses Association.

Jonik. © 2001 by John Jonik. Reprinted with permission.

By September 2000, HCWH had commitments from a dozen major retail stores, including Rite-Aid, Brooks, Albertson's, Wal-Mart, K-Mart, Walgreens, CVS, Toys "R" Us and Drugstore.com. Collectively, the retailers sell millions of thermometers a year.

That kind of market power was enough to get Becton, Dickinson and Co., one of the largest makers of private label thermometers, to announce at the same time that it would stop making glass mercury-based thermometers at its plant in Brazil and stop purchasing them from a Chinese factory.

## The Vinyl Solution

Another HCWH goal has been to reduce the use of PVC plastic in medical supplies, and "to build momentum for a broader PVC phase-out campaign."

"In the late 1950s and early 1960s, when it became apparent that cigarette smoking was the main cause of lung cancer, physicians and nurses who were convinced to stop smoking had an important influence on the general population," says Peter Orris, a professor of internal and preventive medicine at the University of Illinois. "In the same way, as the health care industry begins to act on the connection between dioxin and PVC it will have an important effect on the general public's perception of the issue."

"Mercury was the wedge issue," says Bill Ravanesi, HCWH's Boston coordinator. "Now we're using the credibility built around that to create awareness about PVC and other issues."

Armed with reports on the toxic effects of PVC, HCWH gathered resolutions from a variety of professional associations and state and local medical societies. At the same time, the campaign approached hospital supply purchasing groups such as Kaiser, Tenet Healthcare and Universal Health Services, which have since either stopped buying some PVC products or developed a purchasing preference for non-PVC products.

Meanwhile, HCWH began working with shareholder activists to convince Baxter International, the largest maker of IV equipment and other medical products, to develop timetables to phase out use of PVC.

From the start, the Chlorine Chemistry Council/Vinyl Institute (CCC-VI) lobbied against virtually every HCWH initiative against the use of PVC, often bogging the campaign down in arcane scientific debates which HCWH activists say distracted from the search for safer, cost-effective substitutes.

Some of the industry's efforts seemed to backfire. At the end of 1998, after a number of European countries had enacted restrictions on the use of PVC in toys because of toxic additives that leached out during their use, the CCC-VI, forseeing an effect on U.S. markets, initiated a $1 million ad campaign highlighting the use of PVC in medicine. The pro-PVC ads, which ran in the Washington Post and other influential papers, depicted a group of doctors and nurses in an operating room along with PVC equipment. "People who save lives for a living depend on vinyl," the ads crowed.

The ads motivated HCWH members to investigate the hazards of toxic additives (e.g. DEHP softeners) which leach out of PVC medical devices. What they found was startling and added compelling justification to a PVC phase-out.

Although DEHP had been voluntarily removed from use in toys, it had not been removed from vinyl medical products, some of which (e.g. IV bags) leached the chemicals out in much greater amounts. Evidence from the manufacturers' product labels as well as the scientific literature revealed that some drugs accelerated the leaching process.

"When you add it all up," says Schettler, who conveyed the science to a variety of regulatory fora, "you find that certain kinds of medical care result in patients being exposed to DEHP at or near levels that cause damage in animal tests . . . for example, testicular, liver and kidney damage. Laboratory tests show that the immature, developing animal is most susceptible, and it turns out that some of the highest human exposures to DEHP occur during hospital care of sick newborn infants."

In mid-July 2000, after a two-year study, a National Toxicology Program (NTP) panel expressed serious concern that DEHP may harm the reproductive organs of critically ill and premature male infants exposed during medical treatment.

The NTP finding is bound to further pressure manufacturers of equipment used in neonatal intensive care units, where high levels of phthalate additives may leach and off-gas from vinyl products used in feeding and respiratory therapy.

A breakthrough came in May 1999, when Baxter announced it would "commit to exploring and developing alternatives to PVC products and to developing and implementing proposed timetables for substituting its current containers for intravenous (IV) solutions with a container that does not contain PVC."

As icing on the cake, Baxter also requested that the CCC-VI refrain from using Baxter products in advertising campaigns.

Meanwhile, HCWH campaigners are seeking change from other manufacturers. Plans are being laid for Clean-Med: An International Conference on Environmentally Preferable Medical Products, which will bring hospitals, purchasing groups, manufacturers and academics together in Boston.

"*[Design for disassembly] might cut the
amount of junk that threatens to flood
landfills.*"

# Designing for Disassembly Will Help Reduce Waste

Gene Bylinsky, Alicia Hills Moore, and Karen Nickel Anhalt

In the following viewpoint, Gene Bylinsky, Alicia Hills Moore, and Karen Nickel Anhalt report that manufacturers are now designing products that can be easily taken apart once discarded. The authors explain that companies can save money by designing for disassembly because valuable components of their products can later be salvaged and recycled into new products, eliminating the necessity of purchasing virgin materials. According to the authors, designing for disassembly and reuse also benefits the environment by reducing waste. Gene Bylinsky, Alicia Hills Moore, and Karen Nickel Anhalt write for *Fortune* magazine.

As you read, consider the following questions:

1. As reported by the authors, how did Hewlett-Packard workstation designers in Germany reduce the amount of packaging in which their products were sold?
2. How do U.S. automobile manufacturers recycle used cars, according to the authors?
3. As related by the authors, how did designers at Kodak redesign the company's disposable camera following criticism about the product's wastefulness?

In a big gray brick building in Highland Park, Michigan, a half-dozen technicians and engineers in shirt sleeves are hard at work killing American ingenuity. Armed with air-powered socket tools, screwdrivers, and hammers, they are tearing apart showroom-new cars—a red Ford Aspire here, a blue Chrysler Neon over there. They dissect subassemblies, weigh each component, videotape and time the procedures. Black wire electrical harnesses are removed and hung on tall white boards as if they were the innards of cats on display for a freshman anatomy class.

This most unusual lab is the Vehicle Recycling Development Center, a joint effort of the Big Three automakers that went into full operation in the summer of 1994. Specialists from collaborating recycling associations do most of the demolition, but engineers from Chrysler, General Motors, and Ford visit frequently to observe, often to participate. The aim is to teach the Big Three to better design cars for easier dismantling—for instance, by improving access to key parts for future removal.

## Design for Disassembly

The men and women at the new center are riding the hottest new production trend in the world: design for disassembly (DFD). The goal is to close the production loop, to conceive, develop, and build a product with a long-term view of how its components can be refurbished and reused—or disposed of safely—at the end of the product's life. In a world where the costs of disposal are rising, ease of destruction becomes as important as ease of construction.

The idea has fired manufacturers from Rochester, New York, to Palo Alto, from Tokyo to the tiny village of Uebersee in the Bavarian Alps. Siemens coffeepots and Caterpillar tractors, Xerox photocopiers and Eastman Kodak cameras, American PCs and Japanese laser printers, German locomotive engines and Canadian telephones—plus many other products—are beginning to be built to be taken apart.

The forces behind this newfound environmentalism have more to do with return on capital than with a return to nature. Unlike prior environmental schemes, green manufacturing holds out the promise for companies to do well as they do good. Some American companies, including Xerox and Kodak, are already coining money designing for disassembly and component reuse.

Green machines, with their emphasis on reducing parts, rationalizing materials, and reusing components, are proving more efficient to build and distribute than conventional ones. That's because green production meshes with today's favored manufacturing strategies: global sourcing, design for manufacture, concurrent engineering, and total quality.

## The Green Wave

If that isn't enough, new laws across Europe will soon compel manufacturers of everything from autos to telephones to take back used product. In Germany, the root of the green movement, manufacturers are already responsible for the final fate of their products' packaging.

This green wave of German legislation is rolling across the Atlantic. . . . The Germans have established a de facto global manufacturing standard. U.S. companies wishing to compete globally must start making products that will comply with the green dictates of the huge European market. "Things are moving too fast, with 12 countries already participating in green manufacturing," says Joanna D. Underwood, president of Inform, a New York City-based company that advises corporations on environmental matters.

Green product design could also be the antidote to an astonishing depletion of the earth's mineral riches. And it might cut the amount of junk that threatens to flood landfills in the industrial world. Design dictates a whole chain of events both pre- and post-manufacturing that governs the use, or misuse, of natural resources. Take raw materials extraction, for instance. Judicious use of finished materials like steel could reduce mining demand that totals 20,000 pounds annually for each American. The consequences of this are enormous. According to the National Academy of Sciences, 94% of the stuff that is pulled out of the earth enters the waste stream within months.

European lawmakers are encouraged by the fact that Germany's packaging take-back legislation is working. It has worked so well that the private company organized by manufacturers to collect and dispose of packaging materials has been gathering too much trash—almost going broke in the process because sufficient facilities to remold plastics, for instance, are not in place. But the take-back law reduced the amount of packaging waste by 600 million tons, or 4%, during its first two years of operation.

Although corporations fight such regulations, the green laws in Germany have stimulated companies to develop imaginative ways to market goods with less packaging. Colgate, for instance, designed a toothpaste tube that stands on its head, sans box; it now sells some products that way in the U.S. too.

## From Glass to Concrete

Recycling will gain momentum as we develop materials that are easier to reuse. For example, Jesse Ausubel, director of the Program for the Human Environment at Rockefeller University, predicts that architects will increasingly rely on new types of foamed glass that can be made unusually strong but still lightweight. Glass is a very recyclable material made from sand, and it can be crushed back essentially into sand. Ausubel thinks we could see foamed glass replace much of the concrete in today's buildings.

Ivan Amato, *Time*, November 8, 1999.

Hewlett-Packard's workstation designers in Germany literally moved the packaging inside, substituting plastic foam for the metal skeleton that holds interior parts, thus reducing the need for metal inside and for wrapping outside. A polypropylene foam chassis has cutouts for each component so that all nestle snugly. Channels cut in the foam carry cooling air and cabling to connect the components. The new chassis reduces transport packaging by 30%, while disassembly time has been cut 90%. This idea will be applied to Hewlett-Packard's personal computers as well.

Luckily for manufacturers, the main principles of DFD—use fewer parts and fewer materials, use snap-fits instead of screws—also fit into modern efforts to make assembly more efficient, such as concurrent engineering and total quality control. Concurrent engineering brings different specialists into a design team from the beginning; DFD experts fit into these teams easily. And waste is an enemy of total quality management; hence, DFD also fits in here nicely.

Theoretically, anything from a coffeemaking machine to a Caterpillar tractor can be designed for disassembly. The more value in an item, of course, the more sense it makes to reuse its parts.

Some examples follow of how valuable products are being redesigned in the U.S. and in Germany to fit what the Germans call the new closed-loop economy:

## Green Automobiles

Almost everywhere cars are built, efforts are in high gear to make them more suitable for disassembly and to reuse component parts. Obviously, no one wants to make a car fall apart. Cost, customer appeal, and performance still come first. But car companies are changing some of the ways of automaking to enhance autobreaking. BMW estimates that by the end of the 1990s, 20 million cars a year in Europe will make return trips, 250,000 of them BMWs. To put this many cars into reverse, BMW and other German automakers have been setting up experimental disassembly plants and even executing new-car models to learn more about how to take them apart.

BMW's 1991 Z1 Roadster, whose plastic side panels come apart like the halves of a walnut shell, is an example of a car designed for disassembly. One of the lessons learned, says spokesman Rudolf Probst, is that glue or solder in bumpers should be replaced with fasteners so that the bumpers can come apart more easily and the materials can be recycled. BMW is also changing instrument panels. In the past they were made of an assortment of synthetics glued together. Now BMW uses variations of polyurethane, foam, and rubber so the panel can be recycled in one piece. BMW has pushed the recycled portion of a car to 80% by weight and is aiming for 95%. Francois Castaing, Chrysler's vice president for vehicle engineering, says the U.S. will be in that range by the end of the decade. Volkswagen, too, is on the bandwagon and is planning recycling centers throughout Germany.

The Germans could take a lesson from the U.S. and its robust, market-based auto-recycling industry. "Frankly," says Chrysler's Castaing, "I prefer the more natural, more cost-effective way of what happens in the U.S. We don't have to involve the government and to subsidize anybody in any fashion." Arguably the world's most efficient auto recycler, the U.S. already reuses a remarkable 75% by weight of nearly every American car. Cars are first stripped of valuable parts such as engines, generators, alternators, and other components that can be refurbished and resold by some 12,000 auto parts recyclers. Next, the metal carcasses wind up in the gaping maws of some 200 shredders that reduce the metal skeletons to steel fragments, which are shipped to steelmakers to make more new car bodies. This is already a profitable, multibillion-dollar-a-year business in the U.S. But it is also fraught with problems, such as disposing of tires, glass, and plastic. Green manufacturing—thinking these problems through beforehand—can lower recycling costs dramatically and reduce environmental hazards.

## Green Computers

There are probably insect species with longer life cycles than a PC—now obsolete less than 12 months after it leaves the factory, according to scientists at Carnegie-Mellon University. "Seventy million obsolete computers are sitting in the basements of various organizations and will eventually end up in landfills if they are not recycled," says the university's D. Navin-Chandra. "Today two computers become obsolete for every three purchased. By 2005, the ratio will be 1 to 1, which means we should be able to recycle computers as fast as we make them. For this reason, recycling must be treated like any regular manufacturing task."

In the U.S., laws concerning toxic wastes are scaring computer makers and other manufacturers out of their wits. Reason: If their old machines wind up in landfills and commence polluting the ground, the makers are held responsible. So most U.S. computer companies have begun so-called reverse distribution for old machines, especially from big customers. Some big corporate computer buyers are now writing take-back clauses into purchase orders. The users simply don't want to be burdened with storehouses full of obsolete hardware.

Disassembling old computers isn't new. It began a few

years ago, mainly to retrieve precious metals like gold and platinum. These metals were used in larger quantities in the older machines, deposited as paths to connect chips on a board. The boards were then sold to chip retrievers, which resold the chips to such users as toy manufacturers.

Computer makers that can reduce the number of parts and the time it takes to disassemble a PC will profit when the product, like a sort of silicon salmon, returns to its place of origin. IBM, Hewlett-Packard, Digital Equipment, and other makers are rapidly introducing DFD technology across the board. As early as 1991, IBM designed two models of its PS2E both for easier disassembly and lower energy consumption. Now all IBM designers are being urged to switch to green schemes. Hewlett-Packard has used a DFD approach to build all 12 models of its Vectra PC. Each Vectra now contains only three screws, a construction that also allows easy upgrade by users. "Our customers love it," says Gilles Bouchard, who heads Vectra's mechanical design team in Grenoble, France.

## Computer Innovations

Siemens Nixdorf's green PC41, introduced in 1993, contains 29 assembly pieces, vs. 87 in its PCD-2, built in 1987. The green PC is assembled in seven minutes and can be taken apart in four; the older PCD-2 took 33 minutes to put together and 18 minutes to take apart. The new PC also has only two cable connections, vs. 13 in the old one.

For more than three years, in Research Triangle, North Carolina, IBM has been practicing take-back and disassembly at a facility called the Engineering Center for Environmentally Conscious Products. (It might think about disassembling that name.) The computer colossus is evaluating how such collection could be done at minimal cost, or even at a profit, says center director J. Ray Kirby. IBM takes back its old machines in eight European countries for a small fee, as do most other computer manufacturers.

Hewlett-Packard, which has been in the disassembly business longer than IBM, already runs a profitable operation, according to executives there. DEC says its Resource Recovery Center in Contoocook, New Hampshire, is "cost effective." Germany's Siemens Nixdorf, on the other hand, says its recycling is not yet profitable because not enough old machines are being processed.

Hewlett-Packard's record with its workstations is unparalleled. It rebuilds and recycles every machine that's returned. Says Tom Korpalski, Hewlett-Packard's manager of product stewardship for small computers: "In the hierarchy of the three R's of design for the environment, the first two—reduce [the number of product parts] and reuse [the parts]—rank above recycling."

## Green Telephones

When monopoly prevailed in telephony, manufacturers leased telephones and then refurbished and rebuilt them to lease anew. The breakup of the Bell System disrupted this process, since most phones are now purchased rather than leased. But profitable leasing continues in Canada. In a big plant outside Toronto, Northern Telecom breaks down old telephones, puts their innards into new plastic housings, and sends them out again.

Beyond that traditional activity, Northern Telecom is switching to companywide DFD. "We're on the threshold of moving to a new platform that will truly change the philosophy behind our entire product strategy," says Margaret Kerr, senior vice president for environment and ethics at Northern Telecom in Toronto.

AT&T, moving a bit more deliberately, is in the midst of a demonstration project called "green product realization" to generate guidelines for green product design. . . .

## Valuable Lessons

Valuable lessons come from successful green manufacturers. Kodak has moved well beyond the what-if stage.

Kodak learned the hard way. In the late 1980s a group of engineers came up with a disposable 35-mm camera called Fling. The project got lukewarm support from top management because the idea ran counter to Kodak philosophy. Alan Vandemoere, who participated in the project, says Kodak's belief was "that God intended people to buy a roll of film and a camera and use the film to load the camera."

Indeed, Fling went bung. It sold poorly, and its name enraged environmentalists. Vandemoere's group didn't give up. One engineer devised a double lens that enabled the camera to take wide-angle shots. Creating a panoramic view with a $10 camera was novel. They also developed an underwater version and renamed the camera FunSaver 35. The new model soared—but it still ticked off environmentalists. And for good reason: Hundreds of thousands of returned cameras ended up in landfills.

Eager to recycle the camera, the engineers proposed DFD and component reuse. Kodak management yawned. It woke up when a U.S. Congressman gave the company his Wastemaker of the Year Award for the disposables. Recalls Vandemoere: "My phone rang and one of our senior managers asked, 'Remember that stupid idea you guys had? How long would it take you to implement it?'" Not long, Vandemoere said.

By the end of 1990, Kodak had converted the disposable cameras to recyclable ones. The previously ultrasonically welded camera case was redesigned to snap apart easily. The customer would deliver it to a photofinisher, which would return it to Kodak for a small fee. Kodak hired Out-Source, a New York State-sponsored organization that employs handicapped people, to break down the cameras.

In the recycling center, the covers and the lenses are removed. Plastic parts are ground into pellets and molded into new camera parts. The camera's interior—its moving parts and electronics—are tested and reused up to ten times. By weight, 87% of a camera is reused or recycled. Kodak sold about 30 million disposable cameras worldwide in 1993. The flash version of the FunSaver is the company's fastest-growing and most profitable product. . . .

As Kodak and other companies have learned, the topsy-turvy world of DFD suddenly turns the gang in the lab into corporate strategists. It challenges them to take a much wider view of design than they've been taught. The most important lesson learned, says Donald Bloyer, a Hewlett-Packard senior product design engineer with 27 years experience, is not to be rigid. Coping with sometimes contradictory notions and demands, a designer must juggle quality and reliability with green engineering. In building its popular DeskJet printers for disassembly, Hewlett-Packard found, for instance, that a snap-fit—one of the icons of DFD—just doesn't always work best, so it uses standardized screws instead. It's pointless and wasteful to make a green product that's no good.

Recycling has brought another interesting fact to light: Used or refurbished parts sometimes work better than new ones. This is particularly true in digital electronics. A memory chip or a microprocessor, unless it has suffered repeated thermal insults or physical damage, is virtually immortal, since the only moving parts are electrons. So Fox Electronics, a fast-growing San Jose reclaimer and reseller of chips, doesn't even bother to test old chips it resells. The reason: What the trade calls "infant mortality" of new chips during initial tests is 5%, but Fox discovered that old chips are more reliable—only 2% die.

But old beliefs die even harder. Cheap cameras notwithstanding, getting Americans to buy retread products as new will be a tough sell. Xerox is meeting some resistance to selling or leasing refurbished photocopiers as new, even though they carry the same warranty as machines with all new parts. Car buyers will likely balk at a new car with a refurbished alternator. It's one thing to buy a new Ford with 50 reground plastic soda bottles making up its grille liner. But it's another to accept a used part—refurbished or not—that moves or rotates and wears down with use.

"We still have some educating to do," concedes Xerox's Jack C. Azar, corporate manager for environmental design and resources conservation. "There are pockets in the consumer base—and that includes government agencies—that keep saying, 'We only want 100% new products.'" Azar is pleased that late in 1993 the Clinton Administration, in an end run around Congress, issued an executive order that urges (but doesn't require) federal agencies to buy green products like refurbished photocopiers.

No one knows how many of today's products are green. Maybe 5%, maybe 10%. But in ten years, predicts IBM's Kirby, all products will be made for disassembly and refurbishing—turning both the earth and some companies a greener shade.

> "Recycling [plastic waste]—the least
> practiced [method for disposing of it]—may
> benefit from a new technology that
> promises to make it a more economically
> attractive alternative."

# New Plastics Sorting Technology Will Reduce Waste

Conard Holton

Conard Holton is a contributing correspondent for *Environmental Health Perspectives*, a journal of the National Institute of Environmental Health Sciences. In the following viewpoint, Holton describes a new selective dissolution technology that will help make plastics easier to recycle. He claims that conventional recycling centers use plastics sorting procedures that are labor-intensive and expensive. In contrast, selective dissolution technology enables workers to melt all types of plastic into one solution, then apply heat in order to separate out the six plastic types, each of which dissolves at a different temperature.

As you read, consider the following questions:
1. According to Holton, what kinds of problems are created when plastics are landfilled?
2. What reasons does Jerry Lynch give to explain why recycling is a tough business, as related by the author?
3. As reported by Holton, what concerns does Joseph Visalli have concerning the viability of selective dissolution technology?

As plastics play an increasing role in packaging and consumer products, they also take up a growing percentage of municipal solid waste streams and pose environmental challenges. Once in the waste stream, the plastics are dealt with in one of three ways: incineration, burial, or recycling. Recycling—the least practiced of the three—may benefit from a new technology that promises to make it a more economically attractive alternative.

## Problems with Incineration and Landfilling

Incineration is used to dispose of over 16% of all municipal wastes. More than two-thirds of the incinerators in the United States burn garbage in waste-to-energy facilities that use heat energy to generate steam or electricity. Because plastics are typically derived from petroleum or natural gas, they can generate almost as much energy as fuel oil, although the much higher amount of energy initially required to produce the plastic is lost. Potential hazardous emissions from incinerating plastics include hydrogen chloride, dioxin, cadmium, and fine particulate matter. Even with recent, stricter air pollution standards there is considerable public opposition to incineration.

Landfilling plastics is generally a benign practice because plastics are chemically inert. Some additives to plastics do provoke concern if they should migrate from the plastics into the leachate [liquid produced as garbage decomposes]. For example, heat stabilizers are toxic, but their stability depends in part on the types of plastics and heat stabilizers in use. Heavy metals are being phased out of packaging materials and are a diminishing problem. Plasticizers known as phthalates are hazardous substances and have been found in a number of leachate analyses at various concentrations. A complicating factor in analyzing the leachate is the frequent use of plastic components in leachate collection and groundwater monitoring systems—these components themselves may contribute some of the additives.

A more significant problem for landfilling is that plastic wastes now constitute about 10% by weight and about 20% by volume of the municipal waste stream. Since plastics are essentially nondegradable, their volume will not shrink and plastics may eventually consume a disproportionate amount of landfill space. The Environmental Protection Agency (EPA), in its report *Characterization of Municipal Solid Wastes*, says that plastics comprised an estimated 400,000 tons of municipal solid waste in 1960. By 1994, that figure was 19.8 million tons. The American Plastics Council reports that only 4.7% of this total was recovered, although recovery of some plastic containers has increased substantially. Polyethylene terephthalate (PET) soft drink bottles and their base cups are recovered at a rate of 50%. High-density polyethylene (HDPE) milk and water bottles are recovered at a rate of about 30%. The other common plastics in the waste stream are polystyrene (PS), low-density polyethylene (LDPE), polypropylene (PP), and polyvinyl chloride (PVC).

## Recycling Is Tough Business

Recycling is a four-part exercise of collecting a mix of plastics at curbside or dropoff centers, sorting the plastics into the six types, reclaiming the plastic by physically or chemically converting them to flakes or pellets, and then processing the flakes or pellets into a final product. One reason plastics are recycled less often than glass or metal is because the sorting step is very labor-intensive and, hence, expensive. However, the cost and accuracy of sorting are crucial elements in making plastics recycling economically viable because each type of plastic has different performance characteristics that make it best suited for specific applications.

"Plastics recycling is a tough business," says Jerry Lynch, who manages a project at Rensselaer Polytechnic Institute designed to eliminate the sorting step and reclaim the plastics. "Plastics are contaminated and not easy to wash. They come in different colors and materials, even within one classification. And collection is difficult, meaning that plastics take up a lot of room, and [they] are light and unbreakable, so transportation is expensive. Finally, virgin plastic is inexpensive."

The Rensselaer technology eliminates sorting by introducing a selective dissolution process first developed by Lynch and chemical engineering professor Bruce Nauman. They developed this technology by combining their expertise—Nauman's—in improving the physical properties of polymers and

## Common Plastics and Their Uses

| Polymer Resin | Characteristics | % of All Plastics (1991) |
|---|---|---|
| High-density polyethylene (HDPE) | Tough, flexible translucent | 14.6 |
| Low-density polyethylene (LDPE) | Moisture-proof, inert | 18.3 |
| Polyethylene terephthalate (PET) | Tough, shatter-resistant, gas permeation-resistant | 2.3 |
| Polypropylene (PP) | Stiff, heat- and chemical-resistant | 13.2 |
| Polystyrene (PS) | Brittle, clear, rigid, good thermal properties | 7.8 |
| Polyvinyl chloride (PVC) | Strong, clear, brittle unless treated with plasticizer | 14.5 |

Lynch's in chemical industry processes.

Through a series of processing steps, the unsorted (or commingled) plastics are shredded, washed, and then selectively dissolved in a common solvent. Since each type of plastic dissolves at a different temperature, it is possible to dissolve and remove them from the mixture one type at a time. Alternative new technologies for addressing commingled plastics are depolymerization (an energy-intensive way of breaking polymers into their constituent monomers) and blending (which makes new materials by mixing plastic types but does not yet meet consumer quality standards).

## Selective Dissolution

"In a typical process run on our pilot system, we use unsorted plastic pieces shredded into 3/4-inch pieces," says Lynch. "They get washed to remove impurities, but any remaining contaminants won't cause problems and will be removed later in the process." After drying, the pieces are fed into a mixing vessel along with a xylene solvent at room tem-

| Common Uses | Products Made from Recycled Resins |
|---|---|
| Beverage bottles pipe, cable, film | Motor oil bottles, detergent bottles, pails |
| Trash bags, coatings, plastic bottles | Trash bags, pallets |
| Soft drink, detergent, and drink bottles | Carpets, fiberfill, non-food bottles, containers |
| Auto battery cases, film, screw-on caps, food tubs | Auto parts, batteries, carpets |
| Housewares, electronics, fast food packaging, food utensils | Insulation board, reusable cafeteria trays, office equipment |
| Sporting goods, luggage, pipes, auto parts, misc. packaging | Drainage pipes, fencing, house siding |

League of Women Voters, *The Plastic Waste Primer: A Handbook for Citizens*. New York: Lyons & Burford, 1993.

perature (15°C). "This is the heart of the process," Lynch continues. "At this temperature, polystyrene dissolves upon contact with the solvent and forms a solution of about 6% PS by weight." The polystyrene solution is drained from the mixing vessel through filters to a holding tank, leaving behind the five undissolved plastics. The process is repeated to flush out any remaining polystyrene.

In the next round, hotter xylene is added. "We mix the remaining commingled plastics in xylene at 75°C," says Lynch. "This causes all the low-density polyethylene to dissolve. The low-density polyethylene solution is drained and the cycle gets repeated with increasing xylene temperatures for high-density polyethylene and polypropylene. When only polyvinyl chloride and polyethylene terephthalate are left, we transfer them to a smaller vessel for better mixing and add a xylene/cyclohexanone solvent." The PVC dissolves out first at 120°C and, finally, the PET dissolves at 180°C. The polymer solutions are stored in six holding tanks from which each is moved to a flash devolatilization vessel and a devolatilizing extruder where the polymer is separated from the solvent. All solvent is reused in the process and any impurities are collected for use as fuel, as are any low molecular weight vapors released by the polymers, such as hexane and hexene. The pure polymer is made into pellets and packaged for use.

## Tailoring the Process

Lynch says that selective dissolution also works with the plastics in durable goods such as carpets, consumer electronics, and automobile components. Reclaiming these plastics has been complicated in the past. He notes, "We've worked with Toyota to recycle dashboards. The plastics used in these applications are often combined with something else like a metal part in such a way that you cannot mechanically separate or rework them. The point is, we can tailor the process to fit each situation." In the case of many durable goods, the value of the reclaimed plastics is much higher than that of PET.

"It's basically a plastics manufacturing plant but smaller and cleaner," concludes Lynch. "Conceptually it looks like an oil refinery and it's meant to be built where such facilities are sited." In fact, a preliminary design for a 70 million pound per year commercial plant has been drawn. The capital costs were estimated to be about $33 million, with a profit-making selling price for the recycled plastics of about $0.25 per pound—below the current range of many virgin plastics on the market. However, market conditions in the United States in 1997 are in a state of flux because of a glut of virgin PET, so the economics must be constantly evaluated.

In the Philippines, A. De Vera Corporation recently signed a licensing agreement to build production plants that use this selective dissolution technology. Bruce Nauman says, "Our process makes sense for the Philippines. They now import all their plastic. Recycling provides a raw material they can use to start their own industry." Nauman and Lynch are discussing other licensing arrangements with companies in the United States, Europe, and Asia.

Introducing a new recycling technology means being able to survive in a very competitive industry. "It's a wonderful process," according to Joseph Visalli, the project manager for environmental research at the New York State Research & Development Authority, which partially funded the initial development. "One concern is that it produces a material that is very usable but has to compete against virgin plastic." He thinks that the process may not produce plastics with the specific properties desired—for example, by an end-user seeking to blow-mold HDPE into bottles rather than extrude it for packing crates. On the other hand, he says, "You might not make as many bottles per hour but you pay less for the plastic and the product is okay."

He says, "It's nice because this takes the best route in terms of energy efficiency. You keep most of the energy already invested in the plastic. It's also a good thing that the solvent is reused, but the process is still basically a chemical factory and some toxins will escape. It's very capital intensive and as you get closer to no [toxic] releases you spend more money." As Visalli and others who follow recycling note, plastic manufacturers may not be enthusiastic about this technology since their investment is already made in virgin plastic processing facilities.

The economics of the process is also a question for Cornell University professor of chemical engineering Ferdinand Rodriguez, who has researched solvent dissolution technologies for many years. Echoing Lynch's statement, Rodriguez says, "Recycling is a tough business." He stresses that "Rensselaer's technology is probably one of the most advanced and realistic. But you need to do it on a large scale because economics are a big issue. Recycling is a matter of scale and of educating the public to its importance."

| *"One group has been successfully cleaning up a carbon tetrachloride spill in Michigan using a natural bacteria imported from California."*

# Microorganisms Can Help Clean Up Toxic Waste

Todd Zwillich

Todd Zwillich reports in the following viewpoint that naturally occurring microorganisms have been found eating pollutants at toxic waste sites. However, Zwillich explains that many of these naturally occurring microbes consume waste too slowly to clean up heavily polluted sites such as old nuclear weapons facilities. In consequence, scientists are developing genetically engineered microorganisms that can eat a variety of toxins more quickly. Todd Zwillich writes for Reuters News Service.

As you read, consider the following questions:
1. According to Zwillich, in what ways are researchers taking "a more measured approach" to using microbes for toxic waste cleanup projects?
2. What has kept NABIR from field-testing recombinant bioremediators, as reported by Zwillich?
3. As stated by the author, what problems with naturally occurring microbes have led many researchers to conclude that genetically engineered microorganisms are necessary?

From "Hazardous Waste Cleanup: A Tentative Comeback for Bioremediation," by Todd Zwillich, *Science*, September 29, 2000. Copyright © 2000 by American Association for the Advancement of Science. Reprinted with permission.

After years of relative obscurity, research on pollution-eating bugs is coming of age. But the U.S. Department of Energy (DOE) is not about to field test any genetically modified organisms soon.

## Brave New World

At the dawn of the age of bioengineering, in 1972, General Electric researcher Ananda Chakrabarty applied for a patent on a genetically modified bacterium that could partially degrade crude oil—sparking visions of a brave new world in which toxic wastes would be cleaned up by pollution-gobbling bugs. Researchers quickly jumped on the bandwagon, transferring genes between microbes in the hope of engineering hybrids with a taste for pollution, while a host of "bioremediation" companies sprang up to cash in on the trend. But those hopes were soon dashed. Immobilized by the high costs and technical difficulties of this research, the companies soon went bankrupt. And experimentation retreated from biotech start-ups to government and academic laboratories, where it has remained in relative obscurity.

Now, some 30 years later, bioremediation is slowly and gingerly staging a comeback. Naturally occurring microbes have been tried at a few sites with some limited success. Since 1998, for example, one group has been successfully cleaning up a carbon tetrachloride spill in Michigan using natural bacteria imported from California. Elsewhere, strains of Pseudomonas bacteria have succeeded in remediating halogenated hydrocarbons like trichloroethylene. And in October 2000, the DOE performed its first-ever field test of bioremediation to clean up one of its heavily polluted sites.

With one exception, however, none of the pollution-gobbling bugs released to date has been genetically altered—and DOE is not going to risk it, either. Public resistance to unleashing recombinant microbes—even in field tests—is too great, says Aristedes Patrinos, associate director of DOE's Office of Biological and Environmental Research. Even so, many scientists in this reemerging field, including some at DOE, believe that genetically modified microbes must eventually be employed if bioremediation is ever to succeed.

For the new efforts, researchers are taking what William

Suk, who directs bioremediation funding for the National Institute of Environmental Health Sciences (NIEHS), calls "a more measured approach" than in the past. Then, he notes, microbiologists keen on engineering bacteria to metabolize pollutants quickly learned in lab tests that their bugs had trouble competing with native microbes in their target soil. And those that were effective did their jobs much more slowly than expected.

## A More Measured Approach

Now researchers are trying to avoid these problems by taking into account the chemical properties of the soil and the geological characteristics of polluted areas as well as the properties of the pollution-eating microbes. The DOE effort, for example, will use microbes that emerged naturally from the site they will treat, which is contaminated with heavy metals and radionuclides left over from decades of nuclear weapons programs.

This first field test will occur adjacent to a particularly nasty site at Oak Ridge National Laboratory in Tennessee known as S-3. Now capped by a parking lot, S-3 was once a series of ponds contaminated with radioactive uranium, cesium, and cobalt mixed with mercury and other toxic heavy metals. Without any human prodding, several species of bacteria have adapted to feed on components of the toxic soup that have leached out into the surrounding soil. For instance, these bacteria can transform dangerous metals into less mobile forms that don't dissolve in groundwater. But the natural metabolism of the bacteria is too slow to handle the job, so researchers will add nutrients such as lactate and acetate to the soil in an effort to stimulate the local microorganisms into a toxic feeding frenzy.

"Our ultimate goal is to harness natural processes to immobilize harmful metals," says Anna Palmisano, who manages bioremediation projects for DOE's Natural and Accelerated Bioremediation Research (NABIR) program. If the strategy works, NABIR will next transplant natural bioremediating bacteria from other areas to S-3 to see how well they operate in the new environment.

Conspicuously absent from NABIR's field-testing program are experiments with genetically altered microbes. Although NABIR funds some of this research in outside laboratories, safety concerns, regulatory hurdles, and anticipated negative public reactions are keeping NABIR from considering field-testing recombinant bioremediators "in the near future at all," says Palmisano.

But Oak Ridge microbiologist Robert Burlage and others insist that recombinant technology is exactly what is needed. The problem with naturally occurring microbes, he says, is that "some sites are so bad they will kill off a bacterium as soon as it hits." And no natural bug is equipped to deal with the "witch's brew" of pollutants present at sites like S-3, the way a specially designed microbe could. Deinococcus radiodurans is one example, says Burlage. This "extremophile" is able to thrive under radiation doses of 1.5 Mrads, up to 300 times the fatal dose for humans. But it can't on its own detoxify the other chemicals that often accompany radioactive contamination.

---

## Fungus Helpers

Molecular mycologist Joan W. Bennett claims that the P. chrysosporium fungus "can break down organic toxins, leaving other harmless compounds that other microorganisms use as food."

Bennett wants to use the fungus' might against residues left from munitions production.

The Cold War's end brought closure for many weapons plants, but toxic souvenirs such as TNT (trinitrotoluene) remain.

Medical literature shows it can cause liver damage and anemia. TNT poisons a host of other life forms, including fish, algae—and some kinds of fungi. But if P. chrysosporium proves to be effective, it might help turn back the clock for these former weapon-production sites.

Jill Lee, *Agricultural Research*, March 1, 1997.

---

In January 2000, geneticist Michael J. Daly and colleagues at the Uniformed Services University of the Health Sciences in Bethesda, Maryland, announced in *Nature Biotechnology* that they had transferred into D. radiodurans a gene from the common lab bacterium Escherichia coli that enables

D. radiodurans to resist toxic mercury II. The result was a microbe that could convert mercury II to less toxic elemental mercury, while withstanding high levels of radiation. Daly and colleagues have since added other genes that code for enzymes capable of metabolizing the toxic organic chemical toluene. The researchers wound up with a microbe able to metabolize a heavy metal and an organic toxin in the presence of radiation, at least under lab conditions.

## Fit for a Witch's Brew

At Stanford University, in as-yet-unpublished work, environmental engineer Craig Criddle and colleagues have also designed bioremediating microbes fit for a witch's brew. Criddle's team has taken a gene from a carbon tetrachloride-metabolizing bacterium known as Pseudomonas stutzeri strain KC and transferred it into a heavy-metal metabolizer called Shewanella oneidensis. Now, says Criddle, they have a recombinant strain that can both degrade carbon tetrachloride and immobilize heavy metals. But there's a catch: In lab tests, when the strain metabolizes carbon tetrachloride, it leaves behind chloroform—"and that can leave you worse off than you were before," says Criddle. So that's the next problem his team is tackling, with funding from NIEHS.

At Michigan State University in East Lansing, James Tiedje is trying a combination approach to degrade polychlorinated biphenyls, or PCBs. He starts with a natural bacterium that can consume PCBs. Then he adds genetically altered strains of two other bacteria, Rhodococcus RHA1 and Burkholderia LB400, both designed to remove chlorine and break the phenyl rings in PCBs. The mop-up effort by the engineered strains "can remove the majority of the remaining PCBs, but not all" in lab tests, says Tiedje about his as-yet-unpublished work.

In theory, says Tiedje, these PCB-eating bacteria should be ready for field-testing "by the next warm season," when they would be most effective. But strict regulations on recombinant bugs mean that these and other engineered microbes are unlikely to see the light of day anytime soon. The Environmental Protection Agency must approve any field tests of recombinant organisms. So far, out of 35 recombinant microbes approved for a variety of agricultural and other uses, only one bioremediator—a Pseudomonas species that fluoresces when it contacts naphthalene—has made the grade.

Suk of NIEHS and Burlage chafe at the sluggish pace with which the field is moving; in particular, they would like DOE and other funding agencies to push harder to bring recombinant bacteria to the field. "There are plenty of toxic waste sites far away from population centers that would be ideal for testing," asserts Suk. "Those are the sites to do demonstration research. We need to take some chances to restore [toxic sites] faster, better, and cheaper than we are now."

But DOE, which has some 3000 sites to clean up, is not budging. Says Patrinos: "If we rush into field-testing of recombinant microbes and it fails, we may be worse off in the long run."

# Periodical Bibliography

The following articles have been selected to supplement the diverse views presented in this chapter.

| | |
|---|---|
| Ivan Amato | "Can We Make Garbage Disappear?" *Time*, 1999. |
| Trevor Boyer | "It's Getting Easier to Be Green: Automakers Set Higher Targets for Recycling," *Ward's Auto World*, September 1, 1999. |
| Janice Canterbury | "Designing a Rate Structure for Pay-As-You-Throw," *Public Works*, May 1999. |
| G.W. Dickerson | "Sold Waste: Trash to Treasure in an Urban Environment," *New Mexico Journal of Science*, November 1999. |
| Anita Hamilton-Endicott | "How Do You Junk Your Computer?" *Time*, February 12, 2001. |
| Mike Ewall | "Primer on Landfill Gas as 'Green' Energy," www.penweb.org/issues/energy/green4.html, February 22, 2000. |
| Peter Gorrie | "Cracking the Code: Water from Wastes," *Canadian Geographic*, March/April 1997. |
| Jill Lee | "Microbes Clean Up Toxic Waste," *Agricultural Research*, March 1, 1997. |
| Barbara Marquand | "Hospitals Find New Ways to Keep Reducing Waste," *Sacramento Business Journal*, October 6, 2000. |
| Brian McAndrew | "'Green Torpedo' the Future of Garbage," *Toronto Star*, October 1, 2001. |
| Dick Russell | "Health Problem at the Health Care Industry," *Amicus Journal*, Winter 2000. |
| Megan Smith | "Congressional Testimony: Forest Fuels," Federal Document Clearing House, April 3, 2001. |
| Mark Taitz | "Don't Get Stuck on Medical Waste," *World Wastes*, July 1997. |

# For Further Discussion

## Chapter 1

1. Arthur H. Purcell contends that more needs to be done to avert a garbage crisis, whereas Marian R. Chertow argues that the garbage crisis has already been averted. Examine the evidence that each author provides to construct his or her argument. Which author do you think is most convincing? Cite specifics from each argument to make your case.

2. Bud Angst claims that stringent government monitoring systems make sure that modern landfills are operated safely. However, Peter Montague maintains that landfills contaminate the areas surrounding them and threaten the health of nearby residents. Do you think that private agencies operating landfills would continue to operate them if they had proof that they presented a health risk to nearby residents? Please explain your answer.

3. Paul E. Kanjorski contends that interstate garbage shipping is harmful because it allows polluting states to dump their garbage in other states without having to implement more effective waste management plans. In your opinion, do problems that are "out of sight" tend to become "out of mind" as well? That is, if the effects of a problem are not immediately felt, do individuals have incentive to develop solutions to those problems? Cite specific problems you are familiar with to help develop your answer.

## Chapter 2

1. Sam Martin contends that many individuals recycle because it makes them feel as though they are helping the environment. However, Robert Lilienfeld and William Rathje maintain that recycling may make people feel good but it does nothing to solve environmental problems, which are caused by over-consumption. In your opinion, can individual efforts to better the world effect positive change? Or, do such efforts simply make individuals feel good? Use one or two examples of individual efforts, such as recycling, to develop your answer.

2. Clark Wiseman asserts that recycling costs communities more money than landfilling does. On the contrary, Allen Hershkowitz argues that in the long run, recycling is more cost-effective than landfilling because it creates fewer environmental, social, and health costs. Do you think that the relative value of various waste disposal methods should be evaluated in strict economic terms or should communities consider other long-term

impacts—such as pollution—when deciding which option to pursue? Please explain your answer.

3. Doug Bandow claims that mandatory recycling programs should be abolished because they are expensive and wasteful. On the other hand, William J. Cohen contends that mandatory recycling programs succeed in diverting away from landfills a large portion of solid waste, which can then be processed for resale. In your opinion, what are the advantages and disadvantages of having governments mandate environmental programs such as recycling? What are the advantages and disadvantages of allowing corporations to voluntarily respond to public concerns about the environment?

## Chapter 3

1. R. Allan Freeze describes unsuccessful remediation methods in order to support his argument that toxic waste cleanup projects usually fail. In contrast, the U.S. Environmental Protection Agency discusses various positive indicators to argue that toxic waste cleanup projects often succeed. In your opinion, which author uses evidence more convincingly? Why?

2. Greenpeace asserts that nuclear waste threatens the environment and human health. On the other hand, the Nuclear Energy Institute claims that nuclear waste does not pose a threat because the small quantities that exist are handled with extreme care. The issue of nuclear waste generates strong feelings in most people, which can make the objective evaluation of arguments such as these difficult. Examine your own feelings about nuclear waste. From what sources have you obtained information about nuclear power and its byproducts? Do you feel confident that you fully understand the issue? After examining your feelings, do you believe that you can objectively evaluate the views of Greenpeace and the Nuclear Energy Institute?

3. S.Y. Chen contends that recycling radioactive metal is less costly and harmful than disposing of it. However, David E. Adelman maintains that radioactive metal recycling would endanger human health because the recycling industry could not be adequately monitored for safety. Do you trust the federal government and its agencies to properly regulate and supervise the radioactive metal recycling industry? Why or why not? How did the arguments of Chen and Adelman influence your position, if at all?

4. Most homeowners would think nothing of opening a bag of fertilizer—which likely contains animal dung—for use in home

gardens, but might not be so complacent if the bag contained human waste. In your opinion, why might people accept using animal waste as fertilizer but be strongly opposed to using human waste?

## Chapter 4

1. Charlie Cray reports that companies manufacturing plastic IV bags have tried to block efforts to reduce the use of their products in hospitals even though they are thought to endanger human health. Does the evidence that Cray provides against the plastics industry convince you that plastics manufacturers are acting irresponsibly? Please explain your answer.

2. Gene Bylinsky, Alicia Hills Moore, and Karen Nickel Anhalt report that the German government requires manufacturers to design products for disassembly and reuse. The author explains that companies in the United States have begun to adopt similar designs without government mandates, in part because they want to maintain a "green" image. In your opinion, have U.S. companies gone far enough to reduce waste and protect the environment? When constructing your answer, please discuss specific companies you are familiar with and/or those discussed by Bylinsky.

3. Conard Holton describes new plastics sorting technology that may make plastics easier to recycle. At the end of his article, Holton includes quotes by a professor and a project manager who are concerned about the limitations of such technology. In your opinion, does the inclusion of these opposing points of view convince you that the new technology will fail? Please explain.

4. Todd Zwillich reports that scientists are developing genetically engineered microbes that can eat toxic waste. After examining the information provided by Zwillich about these microbes, do you think such organisms are beneficial? When constructing your answer, discuss both the pros and cons of using genetically engineered microorganisms to clean up toxic waste sites.

# Organizations to Contact

The editors have compiled the following list of organizations concerned with the issues debated in this book. The descriptions are derived from materials provided by the organizations. All have publications or information available for interested readers. The list was compiled on the date of publication of the present volume; names, addresses, phone and fax numbers, and e-mail and Internet addresses may change. Be aware that many organizations take several weeks or longer to respond to inquiries, so allow as much time as possible.

**American Council on Science and Health (ACSH)**
1995 Broadway, 2nd Fl., New York, NY 10023-5860
(212) 362-7044 • fax: (212) 362-4919
website: www.acsh.org
ACSH is an association of scientists and doctors concerned with public health. It seeks to educate the public about what it believes is the exaggerated danger from exposure to chemicals. ACSH's publications include the semiannual *Media Updates* and *News from ACSH* as well as the quarterly magazine *Priorities*.

**Cato Institute**
1000 Massachusetts Ave. NW, Washington, DC 20001-5403
(202) 842-0200 • fax: (202) 842-3490
e-mail: cato@cato.org • website: www.cato.org
The Cato Institute is a libertarian public policy research foundation dedicated to limiting the role of government and protecting individual liberties. The institute publishes the quarterly magazine *Regulation*, the bimonthly *Cato Policy Report*, and numerous books, including *Through Green-Colored Glasses: Environmentalism Reconsidered*.

**Center for Waste Reduction Technologies**
3 Park Ave., New York, NY 10016-5991
(212) 591-7424 • fax: (212) 591-8895
e-mail: cwrt@aiche.org • website: www.aiche.org
CWRT comprises corporations, government agencies, academicians, and other individuals who are interested in promoting public awareness of waste reduction technologies. The center identifies areas for research, conducts educational programs, and facilitates the exchange of information. It publishes the monthly *Aiche Journal*.

## Citizens for a Better Environment (CBE)
407 S. Dearborn St., Suite 1775, Chicago, IL 60605
website: www.cbemw.org

Founded in 1971, CBE's attorneys, scientists, policy analysts, engineers, and community organizers have developed strategies for improving and protecting environmental quality. CBE lobbyists work for more comprehensive regulation of toxic wastes and the protection of sites under threat from pollution. CBE publishes a quarterly newsletter, *The Environmental Review*.

## Clean Sites, Inc.
901 N. Washington St., Suite 604, Alexandria, VA 22314
(703) 739-1200
e-mail: cleansites@aol.com • website: www.cdclark.com/cleansites

Clean Sites is a private, nonprofit organization dedicated to helping government agencies, private companies, and communities evaluate hazardous waste cleanup technologies and deal with contaminated sites.

## Coalition for Responsible Waste Incineration (CRWI)
1752 N St. NW, Suite 800, Washington, DC 20036
(202) 452-1241 • fax: (202) 887-8044
website: www.crwi.org

The coalition promotes responsible incineration of industrial waste as part of an overall waste management strategy. It publishes the CRWI Information Kit, which supplies technical, safety, health, and environmental information concerning waste incineration.

## Environment Canada
10 Wellington St., Hull, Quebec, K1A 0H3 Canada
(819) 997-2800
website: www.ec.gc.ca

Environment Canada is a department of the Canadian government whose goal is to achieve sustainable development in Canada through environmental protection and conservation. It publishes reports and fact sheets on a variety of environmental issues.

## Environmental Defense Fund (EDF)
257 Park Ave. South, New York, NY 10010
(212) 505-2100 • fax: (212) 505-0892
website: www.edf.org

The fund is a public interest organization of lawyers, scientists, and economists dedicated to the protection and improvement of environmental quality and public health. It publishes the bimonthly *EDF Letter* and the report "Plastics Recycling: How Slow Can It Grow."

## Greenpeace USA
1436 U St. NW, Washington, DC 20009
(800) 326-0959 • fax: (202) 462-4507

Greenpeace opposes nuclear energy and the use of toxic chemicals and supports wildlife preservation. It uses controversial direct-action techniques and strives for media coverage of its actions in an effort to educate the public. It publishes the quarterly magazine *Greenpeace*.

## The Heritage Foundation
214 Massachusetts Ave. NE, Washington, DC 20002
(202) 546-4400 • fax: (202) 544-2260
e-mail: pubs@heritage.org • website: www.heritage.org

The Heritage Foundation is a conservative think tank that supports the principles of free enterprise and limited government in environmental matters. Its publications, such as the quarterly magazine *Policy Review*, include studies on environmental regulations and government policies.

## INFORM
120 Wall St., New York, NY 10005
(212) 361-2400
website: www.informinc.org

An independent research and education organization that examines the effect of business practices on the environment and on human health. INFORM research into toxic waste was used as the basis of the U.S. Environmental Protection Agency's national database known as the Toxic Release Inventory. The group's reports and recommendations are used by government, industry, and environmental leaders to solve environmental problems. *INFORM Reports* is the group's quarterly newsletter.

## National Recycling Coalition (NRC)
1727 King St., Suite 105, Alexandria, VA 22314
(703) 683-9025 • fax: (703) 683-9026
website: www.nrc-recycle.org

NRC advocates the recovery, reuse, and conservation of materials and energy. It seeks to encourage recycling efforts through changes in national policies on energy, waste management, taxes, and transportation. The coalition publishes numerous reports and articles, as well as the bimonthly newsletter *NRC Connection*.

**National Solid Wastes Management Association (NSWMA)**
4301 Connecticut Ave. NW, Suite 300, Washington, DC 20008
(202) 244-4700 • fax: (202) 966-4818
website: www.nswma.org

NSWMA is a trade association representing private sector companies involved in garbage collection, recycling, and the disposal of hazardous and medical wastes. It lobbies for laws that are environmentally sound but that still allow communities to dispose of their waste. It publishes the monthly magazine *Waste Age: The Authoritative Voice of Waste Systems and Technology*, the biweekly newsletter *Recycling Times*, and the fact sheets *Waste Products Profiles*.

**Natural Resources Defense Council (NRDC)**
40 W. 20th St., New York, NY 10011
(212) 727-2700 • fax: (212) 727-1773
website: www.nrdc.org

The council is an environmental group of lawyers and scientists who conduct litigation and research on toxic waste and other environmental hazards. NRDC publishes pamphlets, brochures, reports, books, and the quarterly *Amicus Journal*.

**Nuclear Energy Institute (NEI)**
1776 I St. NW, Suite 400, Washington, DC 20006-3708
(202) 739-8000 • fax: (202) 785-4019
e-mail: webmaster@nei.org • website: www.nei.org

NEI is the policy organization of the nuclear energy and technologies industry. NEI's objective is to ensure the formation of policies that promote the beneficial uses of nuclear energy and technologies in the United States and around the world. NEI publications include the brochure *Forging America's Energy Future: The Vital Role of Nuclear Energy* and the online document *From Renaissance to Reality: Vision 2020*.

**Political Economy Research Center (PERC)**
502 S. 19th Ave., Suite 211, Bozeman, MT 59715
(406) 587-9591
website: www.perc.org

PERC is a research and education foundation that focuses primarily on environmental and natural resource issues. It emphasizes the advantages of free markets and the importance of private property rights regarding environmental protection. PERC's publications include the newsletter *PERC Reports* and papers in the PERC Policy Series.

**Reason Foundation**
3415 S. Sepulveda Blvd., Suite 400, Los Angeles, 90034
(310) 391-2245
website: www.reason.org
The Reason Foundation is a national research and education organization that explores and promotes public policy based on rationality and freedom. The Reason Foundation's public policy think tank—the Reason Public Policy Institute—promotes choice, competition, and a dynamic market economy as the foundation for human dignity and progress. The Reason Foundation publishes the monthly *Reason Magazine* and the online *Reason Report* as well as many books including *Earth Report 2000*.

**U.S. Environmental Protection Agency (EPA)**
401 M St. SW, Washington, DC 20460
(202) 260-2090
website: www.epa.gov
The EPA is the government agency charged with protecting human health and safeguarding the natural environment. It works to protect Americans from environmental health risks, enforce federal environmental regulations, and ensure that environmental protection is an integral consideration in U.S. policy. The EPA publishes many reports, fact sheets, and educational materials.

# Bibliography of Books

Frank Ackerman | *Why Do We Recycle? Markets, Values, and Public Policy.* Washington, DC: Island Press, 1996.

Ronald Baily, ed. | *Earth Report 2000: Revisiting the True State of the Planet.* New York: McGraw-Hill, 2000.

Donald L. Barlett and James B. Steele | *Forevermore: Nuclear Waste in America.* New York: W.W. Norton, 1986.

Harold C. Barnett | *Toxic Debts and the Superfund Dilemma.* Chapel Hill: University of North Carolina Press, 1994.

Sharon Beder | *Global Spin: The Corporate Assault on Environmentalism.* White River Junction, VT: Chelsea Green, 1998.

Lester R. Brown et al. | *State of the World 2000.* New York: W.W. Norton, 2000.

Phil Brown with Edwin J. Mikkelsen and Jonathan Harr | *No Safe Place: Toxic Waste, Leukemia, and Community Action.* Berkeley: University of California Press, 1997.

Mark Crawford | *Toxic Waste Sites: An Encyclopedia of Endangered America.* Santa Barbara, CA: ABC-CLIO, 1997.

Ronald L. Crawford and Don L. Crawford | *Bioremediation: Principles and Applications.* New York: Cambridge University Press, 1996.

Richard A. Denison and John Ruston | *Recycling and Incineration: Evaluating the Choices.* Washington, DC: Island Press, 1990.

Dan Fagin and Marianne Lavelle | *Toxic Deception: How the Chemical Industry Manipulates Science, Bends the Law, and Endangers Your Health.* Secaucus, NJ: Birch Lane Press, 1996.

Carl Frankel | *In Earth's Company: Business, Environment, and the Challenge of Sustainability.* Philadelphia: New Society, 1998.

R. Allan Freeze | *The Environmental Pendulum: A Quest for the Truth About Toxic Chemicals, Human Health, and Environmental Protection.* Berkeley: University of California Press, 2000.

Michael Gerrard | *Whose Backyard, Whose Risk: Fear and Fairness in Toxic and Nuclear Waste Siting.* Cambridge, MA: MIT Press, 1994.

Richard Hofrichter, ed. | *Toxic Struggles: The Theory and Practice of Environmental Justice.* Philadelphia: New Society, 1993.

| Valerie Kuletz | *The Tainted Desert: Environmental and Social Ruin in the American West*. New York: Dimensions, 1998. |
| Robert Lilienfeld and William Rathje | *Use Less Stuff: Environmental Solutions for Who We Really Are*. New York: Ballantine, 1998. |
| Herbert F. Lund and William D. Ruckelshaus, eds. | *McGraw-Hill Recycling Handbook*. New York: McGraw-Hill, 2000. |
| Robert Maass | *Garbage*. New York: Henry Holt, 2000. |
| Allan Mazur | *A Hazardous Inquiry: The Rashomon Effect at Love Canal*. Cambridge, MA: Harvard University Press, 1998. |
| William McDonough and Michael Braungart | *Cradle to Cradle: Remaking the Way We Make Things*. New York: North Point Press, 2002. |
| Benjamin Miller | *Fat of the Land: The Garbage of New York—The Last Two Hundred Years*. New York: Four Walls and Eight Windows, 2000. |
| Jerry A. Nathanson | *Basic Environmental Technology: Water Supply, Waste Management, and Pollution Control*. Upper Saddle River, NJ: Prentice-Hall, 2000. |
| David R. Powelson and Melinda A. Powelson | *The Recycler's Manual for Business, Government, and the Environmental Community*. New York: John Wiley, 1997. |
| William Rathje and Cullen Murphey | *Rubbish! The Archeology of Garbage*. Tucson: University of Arizona Press, 2001. |
| Dixie Lee Ray | *Environmental Overkill: Whatever Happened to Common Sense?* Washington, DC: Regnery Gateway, 1993. |
| David Saphire and Sharene Azimi | *Rethinking Resources: New Ideas for Community Waste Prevention*. New York: INFORM, 1997. |
| Fred Setterberg and Lonny Shavelson | *Toxic Nation: The Fight to Save Our Communities from Chemical Contamination*. New York: John Wiley, 1993. |
| Susan Strasser | *Waste and Want: A Social History of Trash*. New York: Metropolitan Books, 2000. |
| Hans Tammemagi | *The Waste Crisis: Landfills, Incinerators, and the Search for a Sustainable Future*. New York: Oxford University Press, 1999. |
| Adam S. Weinberg, David N. Pellow, and Allan Schnailberg | *Urban Recycling and the Search for Sustainable Development*. Princeton, NJ: Princeton University Press, 2000. |

# Index